THE
HOUR
A DAY
ENTREPRENEUR

THE
HOUR
A DAY
ENTREPRENEUR

Escape the Rat Race and Achieve
Entrepreneurial Freedom With Only
One Focused Hour A Day

HENRY J. EVANS

Published by Advantage, Charleston, South Carolina.
Member of Advantage Media Group.
ADVANTAGE is a registered trademark and the Advantage colophon is a trademark of Advantage Media Group, Inc.
Printed in the United States of America.

ISBN: 978-159932-295-7
LCCN: 2011945623

This publication is designed to provide accurate and authoritative information in regard to the subject matter covered. It is sold with the understanding that the author and publisher are not engaged in rendering legal, accounting, or other professional services. The author and publisher shall not be liable for your misuse of this material and shall have neither liability nor responsibility to anyone with respect to any loss or damage caused, or alleged to be caused, directly or indirectly by the information contained in this book. The author and/or publisher do not guarantee that anyone following these techniques, suggestions, tips, ideas or strategies will become successful. If legal advice or other expert assistance is required, the services of a competent professional person should be sought.

Advantage Media Group is proud to be a part of the Tree Neutral® program. Tree Neutral offsets the number of trees consumed in the production and printing of this book by taking proactive steps such as planting trees in direct proportion to the number of trees used to print books. To learn more about Tree Neutral, please visit www.treeneutral.com. To learn more about Advantage's commitment to being a responsible steward of the environment, please visit www.advantagefamily.com/green

Advantage Media Group is a leading publisher of business, motivation, and self-help authors. Do you have a manuscript or book idea that you would like to have considered for publication? Please visit www.amgbook.com or call 1.866.775.1696 enry Evans has an extensive background in business, management, marketing and sales spanning more than two decades and has successfully sold millions of dollars of products and services to clients such as the FBI, Executive Office of the President of the United States, Southwest Airlines, Wells Fargo, and down to hundreds of small businesses.

He currently is involved in four businesses and made the leap to entrepreneurship working only one hour a day. He is both Dan Kennedy Certified and DotComSecrets Certified to work with entrepreneurs on direct response marketing strategies and internet marketing strategies that work in the real world for real businesses.

He runs several completely full Mastermind groups and is a dedicated student of direct response marketing and advertising. He brings a diverse background from both Corporate America and independent entrepreneurship and has a passion for getting things done as quickly and efficiently as possible.

Free bonuses with this book

Visit www.HourADayBook.com

As an owner of this book, you are entitled to a *free, three-part video training* and audio recording of this book worth $550. In these videos, I personally walk you through the best resources to use on your journey to business and entrepreneurial success.

This *free* video training includes short, powerful videos where I will share my secrets with you – no theory here, just hard-hitting and impactful strategies you can use immediately that cover:

- A walk through my personal Top 5 online resources for entrepreneurial success

  - You will learn how to leverage your time
  - Perform quick and thorough research
  - Stay motivated even when life and business are bringing you down
  - Systematize your team and operations
  - Stay organized. How to keep your files up to date.

- A secret "best practices" technique that will help you easily maintain life balance and achieve true peace of mind

- Your own copy of the **daily checklist that I've designed and refined over nearly two decades living and winning in the trenches of the real world**

- Ever wonder exactly how to do what everyone says you should be doing regarding testing? I'll explain what you need to know without any fluff in this short video tutorial on testing.

And you'll get the "**Double Your Time Back**" secret I use nearly every day.

All of these resources are *free* and yours just for asking. Grab them now, because I don't know how long they will be available on the website below.

Visit www.HourADayBook.com to get your FREE gifts today.

Praise for
The Hour-a-Day Entrepreneur

"This is a great book all about entrepreneurial shortcuts to excel in business today. Henry was forced into getting things done in one-hour-a-day blocks, and he shares the specific techniques that he used to make that happen in this excellent book. Read and enjoy this book today."

Brian Tracy

Owner, Brian Tracy International

Author of over more than 45 books

"It is my joy to provide this testimonial and endorsement of my friend Henry Evans. Henry and I have known each other for just a short time, but during that time I have seen how he conducts himself and have seen that he has a very good and giving heart to genuinely help entrepreneurs and would-be entrepreneurs.

"I would highly recommend him to anyone who is in need of getting more done in less time. The premise of The Hour-a-Day Entrepreneur is that you can get more done in less time if you focus on your goals and take action. This has worked for me and can work for you in your own business.

"Read the book, and if you get an opportunity to work with Henry or attend one of his live events, don't hesitate to take action."

John Assaraf,

New York Times **best-selling author,** *The Answer* **and** *Having It All*

Seen on *Larry King Live*, **CNN,** *The Ellen Degeneres Show*, **and** *Anderson Cooper 360*

Featured in the blockbuster movie *The Secret*

"An hour-a-day entrepreneur? No, I do not recommend such a thing as worthy ambition.

"Being an entrepreneur is about who you are, not just what you do. However, Henry did, in fact, escape the corporate world and ramp up a successful business with just an hour a day.

"He's the real deal. Most people make woefully disorganized and unproductive use of their time **and talents,** so a well-managed and well-invested hour can equal eight, nine or 10 ordinary ones.

"To that end, I recommend Henry's book as good burr under your saddle."

Dan S. Kennedy,

Marketing strategist

Author of the popular *No B.S.* book series, including

No B.S. Time Management for Entrepreneurs,

speaker, and serial entrepreneur

www.NoBSBooks.com

"*The Hour-a-Day Entrepreneur* is a GREAT way to look at, and approach, the entrepreneurial process. If you allocate an hour a day to getting ready for achievement, you'll eventually spend an hour a day taking achievemnet actions. I love this book and you will too. Buy it and begin learning the steps to earning your independence and your fortune."

Jeffrey Gitomer

author of *The Little Red Book of Selling*

"This book is a must read for people who want to become successful entrepreneurs. Henry's book teaches you the steps and shortcuts that the wealthy use to succeed."

Loral Langemeier,

Four-time best-selling author, speaker and wealth coach

www.LiveOutLoud.com

"Working only one hour a day? What, are you kidding me!?

"That's what I would have said if I did not know Henry…or if I had not seen him build his business from nothing to something working between the hours of 8 and 9 every night for two years straight.

"Henry Evans is one of the rare teachers in the world, someone who actually practices what he preaches.

"Now, he'll show you the principles he used to make it happen. Listen — if you are content with mediocrity, then go somewhere else. But, if you really want to make more, work less, and enjoy life, this is the book for you. Read it, study it, and then implement it. It's just that good."

Ed Rush,

Former F-18 fighter pilot

Speaker and author of *Fighter Pilot Performance for Business*

www.EdRush.com

"This is an important book about **freedom**. The freedom to work for yourself and pursue your entrepreneurial dreams and never be a wage slave again.

"But most important, it's also a book about achieving that freedom with zero risk. Most people think the only way to be an entrepreneur is to dramatically quit your job. In this economy, that's just plain stupid.

"Henry gives you a step-by-step blueprint on how to build your new venture, while still in your job, for just an hour a day. So the day you do quit your job, you're already a successful entrepreneur (which will make your boss even more annoyed).

"Plus, if you're already a business owner and have moved beyond the hour-a-day phase, Henry Evans is one of the smartest marketers I know, and this book is packed with strategies and ideas that can only make you money."

Chris Cardell,

Recognized as Britain's leading expert on entrepreneurial success and advanced thinking. He has been featured on BBC, ITV,

News at Ten and *The Sunday Times*.

www.CardellMedia.co.uk

"Can an hour a day really make a difference in your life? Henry Evans' book, **The Hour-a-Day Entrepreneur**, proves that anybody can create financial success by following his stories of what works and doesn't work.

"The book is fun, easy to read, powerful and unique. Follow these lessons to success! Every serious entrepreneur needs a copy of this book."

Diane Kennedy, CPA,

New York Times best-selling author of *Loopholes of the Rich*,

Real Estate Loopholes and other financial and tax books

www.USTaxAid.com

"Henry Evans is an implementer, pure and simple. He's driven by a 'big why' and focuses his energy on the things that matter most: first, his family. I've witnessed and watched him grow his business almost from scratch in record time. That means more time for his family and what's important.

"If you want to save yourself years in lost time and thousands of dollars in wasted money, pay attention to what Henry says, does and teaches.

"He's condensed the best of the best in a practical, no-nonsense book that's easy to read, easy to follow, and delivers results. Congratulations, Henry, on doing things most people only talk about or dream of (including writing a book)!"

Mike Koenigs,
CEO and chief disruptasaurus
www.TrafficGeyser.com

"As I've come to know Henry Evans and witness his work ethic and personal life ethics, he truly represents *The Hour-a-Day Entrepreneur*. I highly suggest every entrepreneur who struggles with balancing getting more done while having the life they've always dreamed of, read every word of Henry's book."

Bill Glazer,
Marketing Strategist
Best-selling author,
Outrageous Advertising That's Outrageously Successful

"Henry's book rocks! I've spoken to Henry's group, and I've seen very few business coaches who care as much as he does. He put a lot into these pages to help you join the ranks of other entrepreneurs or become even more successful."

James Malinchak

Featured on ABC's *Secret Millionaire*

Coauthor, *Chicken Soup for the College Soul*

Founder, www.BigMoneySpeaker.com

"**Lots** of books cross my desk every day. As a publisher, I rarely find a book that immediately jumps out. *The Hour-a-Day Entrepreneur* contains amazing wisdom that every entrepreneur, business owner, or aspiring business owner must read and absorb.

"This book is an absolute winner!"

Adam Witty,

CEO, Advantage Media Group

"Whether you're already a successful entrepreneur or planning to 'take the leap' soon, I highly recommend reading this book!

"Henry Evans is not only a shrewd marketer and skilled sales professional, he is also one savvy business owner. The valuable business building lessons you'll learn in this book will save you a ton of time and money and make your own journey much more profitable."

Jim Palmer,

The Newsletter Guru

www.NewsletterGuru.TV

"I've been an entrepreneur for 17 years, and I know what it takes to succeed in being an author, being on TV, and launching new products. It takes a lot of work and you have to be super-efficient with your time.

"Henry does a wonderful job distilling what it really takes to succeed and gives some actionable shortcuts so you can get results faster than before. This applies whether you're a current entrepreneur like me or whether you want to get out of the rat race and do your own thing.

"I've known Henry for many years, and he's able to deliver fantastic results — whether it be in fitness or in business. Listen to what he has to say and take advantage of what he's sharing today."

Cindy Whitmarsh,

Star trainer and expert, ExerciseTV

Author of *Ultrafit, 101 Ways to Work Out With Weights*, and *Ultrafit Cooking*

Fitness expert, *Good Morning San Diego*

www.CindyWhitmarshFitness.com

"As entrepreneurs, we find ourselves drawn to the lifestyle of having control over our schedule and time, enabling us to spend more time with those we love, doing what we dream of. But we've all experienced the trap of growing a small business, and the demands it places on us, draining us of the time and energy to do those things we dream of!

"Henry's **The Hour-a-Day Entrepreneur** *is a road map to escape that trap, or better yet, avoid it in the first place."*

Kyle Widner,

President and CEO, Wild Divine

www.WildDivine.com

"*Henry Evans is going to inspire many budding entrepreneurs with this book. When you read it and apply what you've learned, it will change your life. You'll find yourself with more free time, increased financially security, and extreme satisfaction with creating something from nothing.*

"*By making the courageous commitment to devote your life – even for an hour a day – to nurturing your entrepreneurial dreams using the principles found in this book, you will succeed. Henry explains how to make it happen. Study his words and read this book with a highlighter in hand.*

"*I've been following Henry's advice for more than a year now and my business has completely changed – I'm able to work with my ideal clients to fulfill their dreams with custom jewelry and it's allowed me to take more time off to spend with family.*

"*I'm living proof that these principles really work!*"

Vanessa Mitchell,

CEO, Vanessa Nicole Jewels

Award-winning jewelry designer

www.VanessaNicole.com

"*Reading this book is like enjoying a good steak: tender and meaty. Sharing a full life of experiences and presented in a personal way many of us can relate to and also filled with details and information on how to improve your business, productivity and life.*

"*Thank you for the book and the lessons in it. I am refocused and charged up again because of it.*"

Mike Lee,

Master instructor

Featured on the cover of *TaeKwonDo Times*

www.MastersMA.com

*"Just wanted to thank you for an incredible coaching call last week. In 30 minutes, you opened my eyes to a strategy that's amazingly powerful, yet cleverly hidden inside of what we hear and read from the best marketers and world's most influential people. With your guidance, I now know when the character is designed well, you will never know why, other than you'll want to keep coming back for more. Such a powerful strategy if you want **your** message to be heard again and again.*

"Message delivered…message received!!!"

Greg Lake

CEO, The Lake Companies Inc.

www.LakeCo.com

"I knew Henry was an insightful Mastermind Leader, always pulling the best out of us. I had no idea he was an inspiring writer delivering value nuggets page after page!"

Frank Bianco

CEO, Pear Lake Partners

Entrepreneur

"Being a business owner, wife and mother of a 3-year-old and 10-month-old I'm constantly struggling with how can I get it all done and have a well balanced, meaningful life. This book is my solution! There are so many juicy nuggets and tidbits to help me conquer the chaos and find that extra time in each day. Thank you, Henry, for your valuable insight! My husband, kids and business thank you as well!"

Jessie Schwartzburg

Jessie Schwartzburg Events and Consulting

www.JessieSchwartzburg.com

"If there is one major failure of our society and educational system, it is preparing young adults to be parents. You have to draw on your own upbringing, education, morals and values while hoping that you can find a way to instill those in your children. In the early years it is fun, as they are eager learners and, like dry sponges, absorb all you have to teach them. Somewhere in high school they start to drift away to their peer group and develop their own personalities.

"As they do, the parents are often considered the dumbest people to ever walk the planet and who certainly don't understand teenagers. If a parent is lucky, the young adult eventually starts to realize that their parents did have something to offer, did guide them in a good direction, and are an ongoing life source of love, help, friendship and information.

"And if fortune smiles, the parents may be blessed with grandchildren to spoil and love in their older years.

"As I read my son Henry's book, I smile with pride at the wonderful life and business philosophy he has developed and implemented. I would have been a better and more successful business owner with the blueprint he has devised. I can also see that the trials and tribulations of being a parent were more than worthwhile and that the seeds his mother and I planted have grown so very nicely. He has matured into a solid citizen, respected businessman, a good parent, and a productive member of society. A parent could not ask or hope for more."

Henry J. Evans III Cdr. USN (Ret.)

M/V Queen Ann's Revenge

Cruising in North Atlantic waters

"Henry Evans is an expert in both marketing and time management. I've been fortunate to have had him as a teacher, and he has helped my business expand.

"In *The Hour-a-Day Entrepreneur*, he shares his most valuable ideas for business success. And it's an enjoyable read to boot!"

Matt Hedman,

President, The Perfect Workout

www.ThePerfectWorkout.com

"Let me just tell you how much I **love** Henry's new book, *The Hour-a-Day Entrepreneur*. How amazing to learn from someone that has been there, done that, and is willing to teach it to you in such a brutally honest way. It is like he is giving Cliffs Notes to his $100,000-plus education. This book is a must-buy for anyone looking for another way of living to escape the rat race."

Stacey Crumrine,

Founder, Positively Kids

www.PositivelyKids.com

"What I **love** about Henry Evans is that he has paved the way for you and me to get out of the rat race and he genuinely wants to help us do just that!

"His book is both inspirational and educational — a real-life example of what is possible for both on- and off-line businesses. There isn't a single entrepreneur who couldn't benefit from his story, and I highly recommend learning from Henry whenever possible. A rare gem who is always willing share best practices and trade 'secrets' for those willing to put in the time to learn."

Gina Axelson

Owner, Bella Forma Pilates

President, ThePilatesBiz.com

"Ready to become an Hour-a-Day Entrepreneur?

"Then know that the best hour you could possibly spend right now is to set yourself down today with this book ... and dive in!

*"Because you're learning from the master – Henry is one of America's #1 'Get It Done' entrepreneurs, and you'll be learning from the best. But know that he didn't just write about it – Henry did it. And in here he'll walk you through exactly how **you** can do it too.*

"In these pages, Henry shows you exactly what you need to do to start developing (and capitalizing) on your most important asset – yourself. So get started now. Trust me, you'll be glad you did!"

Ron Seaver

President, the National Sports Forum

President, www.SponsorshipSystem.com

"No business owner or entrepreneur will go wrong by listening to Henry Evans and the sage advice found in this practical, easy-to-read book. By following his wisdom and tips (and capitalizing on the huge investment he's made in himself and his business), you're guaranteed to be leaps and bounds ahead of where you'd be if you never read this little gem. Read it, apply it and create your own success!"

Mike Capuzzi,

Author, entrepreneur, and inventor of CopyDoodles

www.MikeCapuzzi.com

"Henry has been an Infusionsoft customer for years, and he knows how to use it to automate his business. I now know why he has been successful after reading this book. Read and profit from what's inside, today."

Clate Mask,

Small-business growth expert

CEO and co-founder, Infusionsoft

"Henry Evans has put the hay down where the goats can get it by distilling for you the 'secrets of the ages' for becoming a successful entrepreneur. By following his advice and taking action for one hour a day every day, you, too, can escape the rat race and live the life of your dreams."

Steve Clark,

Author and CEO of New School Selling

www.NewSchoolSelling.com

"I finished your book this weekend; I have to tell you that it really struck a note with me, especially the part on making fast decisions. I had been on the fence with some decisions that I needed to make, and my wife and I spent the weekend really talking strategy about our family and the business for the first time in a long time.

"If you had hoped that your book would make a difference, it already has.

"And you can quote me on that!"

Dean York,

President and CEO, PhoenixMark.com

"Having read countless books on marketing, time management and business, I can honestly say this was the most applicable book out of all the books in my bookshelf.

"Henry writes like he's sitting down with you for coffee and telling you all the secrets that made him the successful entrepreneur he is today. Act on one of the many nuggets he offers in this little book and see your success grow!"

Amir Karkouti,

Entrepreneur, public speaker, copywriter

"*The Hour-a-Day Entrepreneur* encompasses the simplicity of success by leveraging age-old proven techniques that are often overlooked by novice and experienced entrepreneurs.

"Henry takes things a step further as well by sharing some 'Golden Nuggets'; that could easily multiply your revenue this year."

Michelle Snow,

Professional basketball player

www.NothingButNetProfits.com

"Henry Evans has hit a home run with his latest book, a compelling story about his journey from corporate management to becoming an entrepreneur.

"It's a well-written, balanced book with real-life examples that can serve as a blueprint for anyone on the path to the freedom of becoming an entrepreneur."

Dr. Charles Briscoe,

Author and dentist

www.LaJollaDental.com

"In *The Hour-a-Day Entrepreneur*, Henry Evans has managed to put together the exact blueprint for running a successful business.

"Henry flat-out knows what works when it comes to marketing and building a business and is able to clearly explain what you need to do and how you need to do it if you want to succeed.

"What Henry teaches you in this book will transform your business and your life. The time- management chapter will save you at least an hour a day, if not more.

"I read a lot of business and marketing books, and I consider *The Hour-a-Day Entrepreneur* required reading for anyone who wants to have massive success for their business."

Jon Barrett,

Founder, Solid Marketing LLC

www.SolidInternetResults.com

"The U.S. economy is in a downward spiral, and any recovery is absolutely dependent on the passion, dedication, and business-creating efforts of entrepreneurs like Henry Evans. Henry epitomizes the axiom 'carpe diem' and has taken the steps to creating his American dream in short, focused chunks of time.

"I've read many marketing, business and self-help books over the course of my career, and *The Hour-a-Day Entrepreneur* simply bulges with information I wish I'd been taught years ago. Henry generously shares the practical tips and lessons he has learned along the way in the pages of this book... and the real gift is that everyone has the time, the opportunity and now the resources to be successful.

"Take a couple of hours and invest the time in reading, rereading, highlighting and 'dog-earing' this book!"

Julie Walker,

President, Hailstorm Marketing

www.HailstormMarketing.com

"Henry Evans is the real deal. His transition from traditional corporate guy to entrepreneur has inspired me greatly.

"I've hit my share of stumbling blocks during my personal journey from Top 10 MBA grad/Fortune 500 whiz kid to my own boss. Henry has been there for me at every turn, and my gratitude to him is beyond words. He helped me when I wasn't sure what next action to take, or where to look for experts and resources, and his suggestions have transformed my businesses.

"Perhaps more important, he's helped me with my mind-set. He a master at pointing out – with encouragement and constructive framing – how I might be getting in the way of my own growth and success.

"Read his book, learn from him, work with him any way you can. They only make a few like Henry."

Elizabeth Pitt,

Growth expert

www.DelightMyCustomers.com

"In *The Hour-a-Day Entrepreneur*, Henry Evans packs an emotional punch that'll jolt you into the reality that you can have it all, if you choose.

"Using real-life story after story, Henry gives you examples that are easy to follow and clearly illustrate the philosophies and strategies that will help you achieve your dreams without sacrificing what matters most.

"Anybody can make money, few truly enjoy it. If you follow Henry's guidance and advice in this book, not only will you be happier and more successful… everyone around you will be, too."

Scott J. Manning,

MBA

www.MillionDollarMethods.com

"I am extremely busy and care only about results. Specifically, cash in my bank account. Is this person going to help me attract cash or not? I run a full-time real estate business in one of the most competitive and brutal down markets in the country.

"During this time, after much soul-searching, I invested in Henry's Mastermind group. Within months, I had turned around a foundering real estate business **and** had a complete information marketing business, as well as my first marketing consulting gig.

"There is nothing earth-shattering in this book, but what is earth-shattering to you is that if you do **exactly** what he tells you to do, you will prosper against any odds. Do not discount the 'mind game' stuff, either.

"It can sound weird and 'new age-y' but I can personally tell you after one meeting with Henry, when I was down to my last dollars, literally, he got my head on straight and I booked more than $27,000 of new net income to myself in two weeks. These are verifiable, honest-to-God, real results.

"Sounds outrageous, but it really happened. Read the book, and much more important, **take action!**"

Josh Lucier,
Real estate broker and internet marketer
La Jolla, California
www.MasonicVibrationSecret.com

"*Want to get in the hall of fame of successful businesspeople? Then read this book.*

"*Henry Evans shares his story about a regular guy, just like you and me, who figures out how to get out of the rat race and set records on his own. He gets out and shows you how to do it, too. All without risking your family or current 'rat race' career.*

"*Ever since I've known Henry, he has shown everyday the tactics he teaches in his new book. Henry's steadfast, simple tools and habits allowed him to create a successful business of his own without outside investment and without any bosses destroying his good work.*

"*It's simple, consistent application, just like Henry teaches, that will lead you to the top fame of your field. This book will cut through the noise and start you toward success.*"

Steve Scott,

Professional director and CEO confidential adviser

Host and publisher, Leadership Point Radio

CEO, Technology Acquisition Group

"*If you are interested in breaking out of the rat race, Henry's book will give you the insight and tools that you need to make the move. With his knowledge of business and marketing, and the effective use of time management and focus, he provides a proven path that will guide you on your way.*

"*Read Henry's book and make the commitment to yourself to reach your goals by following the principles and examples that he shares.*"

Doug Brennecke,

Mortgage broker

Author, *Home Sweet Home Loan*; available on Amazon.com

"The old saying goes, 'Don't bring a knife to a gun fight.' Henry Evans would never be accused of that. If anything, over the several years I've been privileged to work with him, I've seen him bring the equivalent of a Gatling gun and Sidewinder missile mounted on an Apache attack helicopter – just to properly deal with a business or marketing challenge! Your business will have its own knife fights. Make sure that the wisdom of Henry Evans is a part of your strategy."

"Coach Gary" Micheloni,
www.BestVideoWebMarketing.com
Author, *Get Paid for a Change!* **and**
Full Contact Project Management

"Henry Evans takes the reader through a true journey of his own experiences with entrepreneurship, and it is through this magical journey that one can truly understand what it is to be an entrepreneur.

"It is very inspiring to read about someone who was in the corporate world but was able to leave that security and salary in order to follow his true passion. You read about successes, suggestions, advice and lessons learned. This is truly a life-changing handbook for anyone with even the slightest inclination toward entrepreneurial freedom.

"If you are contemplating leaving the rat race, or maybe even know someone who is, this book is a **must-read!**"

Christine McDannell,
Managing partner, www.SocialStarfish.com
President, www.AdoptAChristmasTree.com

DEDICATION

This book is dedicated to three people
who motivated me to exit the rat race so I could
spend more time with them –
my two lovely daughters, Arianna and Alexandra,
and my wife of more than a decade, Erin.

My deepest thanks to each of you for all your support
and love. It is a lucky man who gets to live with three
beautiful women, and I am blessed.

I also dedicate this book to you, the entrepreneur.
The future of this country, and of the world,
relies on you taking your ideas to market.
So THANK YOU.

ACKNOWLEDGEMENTS

Many people and books have guided me on my journey to the present success and satisfaction I enjoy in my life. I would like to acknowledge and thank all those people for the experiences and knowledge I have acquired through them. I have listed some of those people below; but the list is not all-inclusive, so if you are not included, please realize that the omission was not intentional.

First I want to mention my parents, Ann and Hank Evans, for raising me in a fun and stable home environment. They are deserving of all the respect and thanks I can give.

I also want to mention and thank the following people:

Rick Lohr, Kevin Crowley and John Mandelbaum for the early exposure of what you can realize when you become an entrepreneur, independent from the rat race that previously had you running in circles and getting nowhere.

Ray Pittman and Kathy Schloessman for guiding me on my journey and being my first two friends from California.

Jim Vargas for showing it *is* possible to have everything – a rewarding, successful career, a strong faith, and a wonderful family.

Jim Fitzgerald for giving me an opportunity to change careers.

Allen Drennan for being a visionary and Stacey Hart for bringing us together.

Scott Tucker for introducing me to direct response marketing. Dan Kennedy and Bill Glazer for drastically furthering my marketing education and increasing my bank accounts.

Ed Rush Jr. for being a great friend and showing me the road to success. James Malinchak for believing in me. Michael Koenigs for his tremendous energy and contagious ideas. Chris Cardell for being a wonderful visionary. Craig Jacobson for his levelheaded expertise. Ron Seaver for the best personal emails I've ever received.

Brian Tracy and Robert Kiyosaki for the hours we were able to spend together.

Of course, I also owe a thank-you to the countless others who have gone before me in making the leap of faith from corporate America into the fun and exciting life of the entrepreneur or who have provided guidance, wisdom or just conversation along the journey.

Thank-you, San Diego, for being the best place to live and raise a family.

And special thanks to those I will be meeting along my way – I know that we will be brought together and I sincerely look forward to our future relationship.

And last, but most important, *thank-you, God, for your countless blessings.*

Henry Evans
January 2012

TABLE OF CONTENTS

FOREWORD

What matters: My story might be a little like yours. This is how it starts: Your parents are telling you that you need to get good grades. You work hard at school to get into a good college. You get out of college and get a "good" job, work hard and hope the company will take care of you through your later years, right?

Well, that's what I thought, just like all the other countless cogs caught in the wheel of misfortune that we call "working for a living" in employment that often leaves little time for a meaningful life. After pouring 14 years of "hard work" into following that well-worn path, I was no further ahead. Actually, I was firmly entrenched in the system with a mortgage, debt and limited savings to go along with my hard work.

It wasn't until I was returning from a long sales trip to Washington, D.C., back to San Diego that I discovered exactly where I was in my life. One of my flights had been delayed, and I wandered in to the bookstore. There, I saw what many refer to as the "purple book" up on the best-seller list. So, I picked up *Rich Dad, Poor Dad* by Robert Kiyosaki and Sharon Lecter and was hooked on just the first few pages. This book was telling a great *story* and that's what caught my interest.

After investing in the book and reading through most of it on the long flight home, I finally realized where I had put myself over the last 14 years. I was firmly entrenched in what they called the rat race.

I was working harder and harder just to stay in the same place.

And I didn't like what the future was shaping up to be. Already I was in my 30s, struggling to pay my bills, trying to get ahead. Now I saw myself ending up middle-aged and stuck in a dead-end job, unhappy and broke.

I can still remember the feeling upon missing one of my daughter's kindergarten events because I was traveling for my job instead of being home with my family. Have you ever had a real sick feeling in the pit of your stomach? That's what it felt like.

Not only did it make me feel bad about myself, but it also filled me with disgust. Why wasn't I able to find the time to be with my daughter on her special day? Because I had made my priority my employer's company instead of my family.

Take 5 minutes...

...and find the thing that matters most in your life *right now.* Hint: it's probably hidden behind that box of reports and the stack of forms and contact sheets and that pile of self-help books.

It might be your wife's or daughter's name. It might be the goal you lost someplace after college. It might be a decision to divorce your credit cards.

Find it and **write it down** on a Post-it, scratch it on the wall, scribble it on your forehead, paste it on your PC monitor. Just **put it in front of you and keep it there.**

That message is **why** you're doing everything else.

WHY WASN'T I ABLE TO FIND THE TIME TO BE WITH MY DAUGHTER ON HER SPECIAL DAY? BECAUSE I HAD MADE MY PRIORITY MY EMPLOYER'S COMPANY INSTEAD OF MY FAMILY.

I wasn't taking care of myself either; I was always tired and was distancing myself from what mattered most to me because of my job and had gained quite a bit of weight from the stress of the entire situation.

Even so, I was in a good situation compared with some…

You could end up fired like my good friend Richard, who at age 55 was let go from a highly paid executive position while living in Chicago. It took him two *years* to find something else. And he was eating up his 401(k) the entire time of his search – not to mention the stress and strain that being unemployed put on his family and personal relationships.

Or like the well-dressed, presentable gentleman I just sat next to on a long coast-to-coast flight. He's currently an unemployed pharmaceutical sales rep looking for a job. He's in his mid-40s, married, with two kids. And he's scared.

No wonder: A good friend of mine who owns a pharmaceutical company tells me that this gentleman is not the only middle-aged, out-of-work pharmaceutical sales representative. There are *lots* of them right now. They, too, are in the rat race – or at least they are frantically trying to get back into it!

For me, almost instantly after I read that book, I decided to exit the rat race and become financially independent. The most important reason was that I wanted to have control over my life instead of giving the control to an employer, somebody else, with the hope that they would look out for my best interests.

Take 18 minutes…

… balance your checkbook and **make a list of your primary assets.**

It seems simple, so simple it's almost not worth doing. But if you don't know how much you've got (or how much you need), your working life and your personal life are both out of control.

Gain control by gaining knowledge. Ignoring your current situation will not help. Little details, overlooked, can become huge, time-eating problems.

Knowing where you are today will help you begin the process. It can be done in just a few minutes. Try it now.

I took this to heart, and the seed was planted. It took quite a while for that seed to really sprout; but later on in my own life, I modified my goal to get myself out of the rat race *by working just one hour a day.*

Why one hour a day? Because that was all the time I had!

We were blessed with two baby girls in a 13-month period in 2003 and 2004, and at that time I also had a full-time job as a software company executive. I didn't want to miss out on family time with my kids or with my wife, and my programming wouldn't allow me to do a poor job at work, so I ended up working from 9-10 p.m. each night on my own business. That was after family time and after enjoying an hour or so with my wife. Then, at that late hour, I would sit down at my PC or at my desk.

I KNOW EXACTLY WHERE YOU ARE AND CAN ABSOLUTELY RELATE.

What's both funny and amazing is that when you only have an hour of time to focus you can get a lot of work done. I actually found I could get more done in my five to 10 hours a week (I usually worked at least a half day on the weekend) than fellow business owners did in a full 40-hour workweek.

Was I four times or eight times smarter than anyone else? Certainly not! But I did learn a few tricks that enabled me to get more done. **I learned those tricks from mentors, books, and strategies I picked up along the way.** And of course, I had my strong work ethic because I had always correlated hard work to success. Through a lot of trial and error, I was able to build up a business utilizing just one hour a day – working every night and usually several hours each weekend.

This book is all about the journey I began many years ago at the moment I decided to exit the rat race and forge forward on my own. Within this book's covers, I offer colorful examples and concrete ideas about overcoming what was, for me, a nearly paralyzing fear of job loss. If you have ever felt stuck or not able to do what you knew you needed to do because of negative programming, this book is for you. **I know exactly where you are and can absolutely relate.** This book holds the key to giving you a positive outlook for your future – in an hour (or less!) every day.

After you get past the negative programming hurdle, you will be able to follow the blueprint I will show you – the same blueprint I used to leverage my experience to find freedom and peace of mind in my life. **You can have that same freedom and peace of mind – I know you can do it because the path I followed has been well-worn by others.** You just need someone to show you the way. Today, that someone is me, and I'm glad to help.

CHAPTER 1

TEN EXTRA SECONDS OF WISDOM:

When you spend time daily
on what's important in your business – work to a
countdown clock and get things done quickly – it will
give you a tremendous productivity boost!

THE CLOCK IS RUNNING

The game is on. Do you want to play or sit on the bench? If you choose the bench, you're playing somebody else's game. This is the time to ask yourself an important question: Do you want to have your own business or achieve entrepreneurial success?

I've read a lot of books while going on my journey from a corporate executive to a self-employed business owner and entrepreneur. It has been a fun and exciting journey. Not easy, but fun and exciting. Being led to many good books and resources has been instrumental in helping me make the shift. But there was never one key thing that helped me put together how to make the transition. There was no overall blueprint or plan.

Take 3 minutes...

...and **find the end zone**. You're already in the game. You'll play better and smarter if you know where the goal is, and what looks like.

Now, choose one simple step that will take you in that direction by describing your goal to another person. It could be an email, a phone call, a conversation with a trusted friend. Saying it makes it real. Putting it in writing makes it even more real.

Be specific or general, but **knowing where you're going is the first step in getting there.**

This book is designed to be just that type of strategy for you; it's designed to give you an overall plan of the changes that need to occur to go from a stable J-O-B into something scary but ultimately life-changing, the freedom-filled world of business entrepreneurship. *Or if you are already in business, this book will give you some tools and specific strategies that can accelerate your success.*

This tale is guaranteed to inspire you. **I've literally put what I know that will help you on your journey to success into the book you now hold in your hands.** Best of all, it's organized to do just that in 60 minutes a day – or less.

Why?

Because **what you are probably looking for is the same thing that led me to choose the entrepreneurial path – you are looking for freedom.** You want financial freedom, freedom from having a job, freedom from being held back by the "system." You want freedom to choose to spend time with those you care about, freedom to choose what you want to do, freedom to choose the impact you want to make on this world.

Take 32 minutes…

And **write your own declaration of independence.**
It'll have three parts:

1. What trap is keeping you from achieving what you desire most? Fear? A big mortgage? Bad habits? Lost confidence? *Name your enemy.*

2. Want to pursue some life, liberty and happiness? A pursuit is a quest. Say how you will pursue those things. Say it like your mean it. Say it like a *promise.*

3. What are you willing to sacrifice for your personal freedom? Make a short list, as the Founders did when they talked about pledging their lives, liberty, even their sacred honor.

But remember when you were asked about *what really matters* to you? (See page 42.) Don't sacrifice *that.*

Looking back, I can see that there were some key things I learned that made a very big impact. Each of these core lessons became shortcuts on my journey. They made my life easier because they illuminated the path of success. Without them I might very well still be working in the rat race.

FOLLOW THE PATH

What I didn't know in the beginning is that **the path to success is very well-worn** and that many have left "bread crumbs" behind that can show you the way to reach success. Although I eventually learned these strategies – better late than never – I wish I had been given them many years ago, because it would have made the transition much easier for me. But I'm happy that I found them eventually and now can put them together in one place – in this book – to make *your* journey easier.

Each of the chapters in this book is about some idea or strategy that made a tremendous impact on my life. While I was living it, that wasn't always apparent. The road to success is definitely not a straight line! In hindsight, I know how important these strategies were to getting me where I am today, and it is my mission to impart all that I have learned to you.

THE PATH TO SUCCESS IS VERY WELL-WORN.

"Books are what you step on to take you to a higher shelf. The higher your stack of books, the higher the shelf you can reach.

"Everything you need for your better future and success has already been written. And guess what? It's all available. All you have to do is go to the library. But would you believe that only three percent of the people in America have a library card? Wow, they must be expensive! No, they're free. And there's probably a library in every neighborhood. Only three percent!"

– The late Jim Rohn,
author, speaker and success coach.

We all look forward to and dream about where we want to go in life. As we reach a milestone of life and turn around to have a look, we see that the journey is not linear. It is a zigzag path of constant course corrections and adjustments, failures and lost opportunities. But if we stay the course, make adjustments, and continually seek the ultimate goal, we *do* find what we are looking for.

If you've ever flown cross-country, you'll notice that on a long flight, you are very rarely right on course. You actually zigzag and course-correct for the entire journey. So a flight going from New York to London is only exactly on course for a short part of the time; the flight direction is actually in a constant state of adjustment, based on the winds, fuel consumption, air traffic, weather systems and more.

Take 24 minutes…

And **make your flight plan** for the next 10 years.

• When will you start? Where will you land?

• Make a line and mark off the years in six-month segments. Pilots need to know fuel and flying time. You need to know income and expenditure.

• Decide your minimum "altitude" – expressed in dollars. Then mark each six-month segment with the altitude at which you expect to be cruising. If you need $10,000 a year to get off the ground, chart it. If your altitude by year three should be five times that (or more!), put it on your flight plan. With luck, you'll be flying higher and landing happier, and your flight plan will be a rising arc of success

Wherever you are at the end of your 10-year flight plan becomes the place you use to take off for the next flight. Money is a tool for you – fuel for your business – to help you climb even higher.

This is just like your life. You need to know *where* you want to go. You must have your destination firmly planted in your mind, and you must be *clear* on what that is and how you're going to get there.

When you have that destination or goal in mind, it makes all of the difference. Why?

Because when you know with absolute clarity where it is that you are going and why, you will discover that as life hands you the inevitable twists, turns, delays, setbacks, turbulence and more, you'll come to see that those are nothing but minor detours on your flight path to success. You'll be able to make those little course corrections and big life decisions that will get you to the place you set out to reach.

A few minutes in the
Place of Honor...with Gina Axelson

Every weekend (usually on Sunday nights), I set aside time specifically to look at the week ahead, review my goals and to-do list, decide what I want to accomplish, and then figure out how and when I can make that happen in the days ahead. For me it seems that every week is different, between family, school and work schedules, so making this simple task a priority each week really makes all the difference!

Gina Axelson,
Owner, Bella Forma Pilates
President, The Pilates Biz

Here's your pocket summary of what we talked about here:

- Find your goal – where do you want to go.
- Write your own declaration of independence.
- Follow the path others have already discovered.
- Set aside time every week to plan the next seven days.

CHAPTER 2

TEN EXTRA SECONDS OF WISDOM:

Essentially, you need to spend some time
each and every day working on YOU and making
yourself better – even if it's just five minutes of thinking
about how to improve your situation or listening
to something positive.

I WENT KNOCKING
AND FOUND
THE BEST INVESTMENT

Find your starting point! There's no better way to know how much progress you've made than to look back at where you've been. For me, that start came one day out of the blue when I had just graduated from high school.

Early summer, 1991: Nervous and sweaty – that's how I was when interviewing, along with a friend of mine, for a summer job back then.

We had just graduated from high school in West Des Moines, Iowa. It was my third high school in four years. Not easy, right! Not fun is right, too! It wasn't easy having so much change at a pivotal time in a young man's life. But now I was through high school and here I was interviewing for a job and – although I didn't realize it at the time –I was about to change the course of my life for the better.

I hadn't expected to graduate from a high school in Iowa. In fact, I had been there for only two years. I grew up in a little town called

Youngstown, New York, with a total population of 1,812. We were only about 15 minutes from Niagara Falls.

To get to this sleepy town where I grew up, you would need to go over the Niagara Falls in a barrel (which is not only illegal, but often fatal). Let's assume that you did survive after you went over the falls and then drifted down the Niagara River in your barrel. Right before you popped out into Lake Ontario (the last of the five Great Lakes), you could look up on the left-hand side and see Niagara-On-The-Lake, Ontario, Canada, and on the right-hand side see Youngstown, New York.

There was a point when I knew all of the attractions at Niagara Falls so well that my mom would tell me to take our guests on tour by myself! So there would be a 10-year-old in the back seat, going through the tour of Niagara Falls for the adults in the front seat. This was always a fun thing to do, and the Niagara Falls area was a very neat place to grow up.

SMALL TOWNS, BIG BENEFITS

I lived in Youngstown through my first year of high school. This was and still is small town America at its best. The parents of my best family friends from my growing-up years still live in that same small town. They were high-school sweethearts, and both of their parents were from Youngstown as well. You just don't hear stories like that much anymore! When the mayor of this small town holds summer concerts in the park, he begins by saying, "Welcome to Mayberry."

Take 45 minutes...

...and **list one friend from every year** of your life from age 5 to age 25. You know what you have. This little exercise will tell you what you may have lost.

Now circle the names of the people you haven't contacted for a while – and **send each of them a message**. With the internet, it's easy! Send them a quick sentence on Facebook. But get back in touch. In less than an hour, you'll have rediscovered something of real value in your life: a friend.

My small-town nirvana ended abruptly at age 16. My father was offered a job and we got uprooted and moved to Flemington, New Jersey – just about an hour out of New York City.

It wasn't easy, but I got excited for the move to New Jersey and had soon acclimated well to my new school and surroundings – even becoming very good friends with identical twin brothers, which would serve me well later, when I married a young woman who had a twin sister.

After my secluded childhood in a sleepy little town, living just a short drive out of New York City was anything but boring. But that, too, didn't last. Only a few months later my father decided that he was going to accept an opportunity to move up in his new company and uproot us all and move to... Des Moines, *Iowa*. Now, this was only nine months after moving to New Jersey!

I distinctly remember my father talking to a retired, successful friend and mentor and getting his advice on a possible move to Iowa. His friend said something along the lines of "Don't say 'no' to any opportunity."

Now, there is nothing wrong with that advice, but one thing I always try to do is take into account who is giving me advice. This gentleman was a career banker, never an entrepreneur and never had kids. As I look back, I believe his input helped push my father over the edge and into moving his family halfway across the country. This was the first time that **I clearly realized how we each make our own decisions** and that I probably would have made a different choice given the same situation.

AMAZING HOW WHEN YOU SAY SOMETHING ENOUGH, YOU REALLY START TO BELIEVE IT.

Nevertheless, I did as we all would do if faced with the same predicament, I adjusted to the new situation. In Iowa, I met some of the nicest people in the world, people who had great family values.

Iowa was a great place to raise kids and a fun place to go to school, but it wasn't the place of excitement I was hoping for. In fact, my 16-year-old mind was so embarrassed that I actually told people at my school in New Jersey that we were moving to Colorado. **Amazing how when you say something enough, you really start to believe it.** When it sunk in that we really were moving to Iowa, I realized that I would have to make the most of the move and adjust to Iowa as I had to New Jersey. (For the record, nobody at my New Jersey high school ever learned that I moved away to Iowa!)

I CLEARLY REALIZED HOW WE EACH MAKE OUR OWN DECISIONS.

So, Iowa is where I graduated from my third high school and where I found myself at my sweaty job interview that summer before heading away to college.

The one good thing about attending three high schools is that it forces **you out of your comfort zone, because it teaches you that in life you have to meet new people and go new places.** It was a hard move for me to leave everything that I had known my entire life and move across the country. As I look back, however, I see that it was one of the best things that happened to me, because it forced me to accept change and make the most of a difficult situation. That turned out to be great early training for business and life.

Take 30 minutes...

...and **connect your dots.**

Make a simple timeline. Draw a line the length of a piece of typing paper. Put "age 18" at one end and "now" at the other. Connect the two points with a straight line. Now make a black dot for every significant event along that line in chronological order. If the event was positive, make the dot above the straight line. The best events should be highest. Not-so-positive? Put the dot below the line. The worst events should be lowest on the page.

Now **connect the dots.** See what this tells you about the choices you've made – and what to look for going forward. And note that you definitely haven't progressed in a straight line; none of us ever do. I'd be willing to bet that some of the points below the line actually helped you achieve some points above the line – funny how that works.

SELLING THE DREAM

So back to my "sweaty" 1991 interview, which was for a wonderful job with a company called Vector Marketing. If you have heard of Vector Marketing, you know exactly what kind of firm it is. If you haven't heard about this company before, Vector is the marketing arm for Cutco Cutlery. It makes what some consider the best kitchen knives you can buy – expensive, but a great product, sold primarily door-to-door, via appointments, by college kids signing up for the "unlimited opportunity" the company generously offered.

They were selling "The Dream"…but **the sales pitch was so good it didn't matter what they were selling.**

Getting hired by Vector Marketing works like this: The first day of your "interview" you go in for a couple of hours to get sold on the opportunity – before you even learn about the product! The company is actually convincing you of the opportunity, because I highly doubt it would have an endless stream of interviewees if the job ad read, "Sell knives on 100% commission to your parents, parents' friends and your neighbors."

YOU WANT ME TO SELL WHAT?
TO MY FAMILY AND FRIENDS?
FOR 100% COMMISSION?
WHERE DO I SIGN!

But everything the interviewers did that first day really got me pumped up! By the time they were done with me and everyone else in that room, **it really didn't matter what we were going to be selling, because we had bought into the dream.**

They were so good, I bet they could have brought out ice cubes as our product and we all would have willingly gone out with smiles on our faces and hawked the product to Eskimos in Alaska!

YOU GET OUT OF SOMETHING WHAT YOU PUT IN TO IT.

When I learned about the actual product we'd be selling, I wasn't dismayed at all. I distinctly remember going out to our cars with my friend Barry after we had been "hired" to sell this product and saying to each other, "We are going to get rich this summer." It was amazing to see how you can get people so excited about the product you are selling once they buy into "The Dream."

To best sell the kitchen knives, you're asked to make a list of everyone that you know. They have you do it as a contest, so you end up getting hundreds of people on your list because you want to win. Then they tell you that you are looking at your new prospect list! So, I ended up calling everyone my parents knew, everyone in our subdivision, and every friend's parents, as well as everyone in my school, in order to get as many appointments as I could.

I had learned a very important lesson: **You get out of something what you put in to it.**

I put in the time, I did what they said, and I was very successful at selling knives that summer. I learned how to deal with rejection; sell one-on-one, nose-to-nose; and for the most part, I enjoyed it. I realized the law of what I put into something, I got back. I really worked hard at getting good at sales, at learning how to deal with calling people who didn't want to talk to me and at being successful at what I applied myself to doing.

The best thing by far that I learned, however, didn't have anything to do with selling knives; and it's **the main lesson** that I want to share with you. This lesson…

Didn't have anything to do with selling.

And didn't have anything to do with marketing.

It had to do with the quote in the first chapter from Jim Rohn. Quite simply, it **was about reading, growing and learning**.

Now understand this: I did fairly well in school – top 20% of my class, worked hard at some subjects (such as Latin) and didn't have to work hard at others (such as chorus). I always did OK in school and was accepted by every college where I applied.

REFERRALS ARE AMONG
THE MOST VALUABLE LEADS
YOU CAN POSSIBLY GET.

I was doing OK for a small-town boy; but I never really developed an appreciation for reading or for learning. I'm not sure if it was because of me, or my parents, or what, but I had never before been exposed to something that I saw for the first time one fateful day in the summer of 1991.

Once I had gotten started with my first few appointments as a salesman of knives, part of the sales script was to get referrals from each appointment for others whom I could call on to give demonstrations. (This showed me the power of referrals from very early on. Today, I know that **referrals are among the most valuable leads you can possibly get** in any business.)

Actually, I hated making cold calls, even though I had an "in" on every call because the people were usually a family friend or a friend's parent or a referral. It was summer in Iowa and it was hot... and it was very, very humid. So it wasn't too bad sitting inside our nice air-conditioned house making a few phone calls. Late one summer afternoon in June, I was going down my list of calls, trying to set up "demonstrations" of the knives. Basically, I was setting up sales appointments. Then something happened that changed everything.

THE "P" LESSON

You never know what you can learn from a smart prospect. Here's a little story about a lucky knock on the right door at the right time.

I was going down the list of everyone inside our subdivision and I came to a strange name that I could barely pronounce, Podhajsky. So I called the Podhajsky house and got Mr. Podhajsky on the phone. (This was the early '90s before there were "do not call" laws; and this was also in the Midwest, so people answered the phone most of the time and would talk to you.)

Mr. Podhajsky, as it happened, was a very nice guy and very agreeable to get together with me for an appointment.

As I mentioned earlier, Vector Marketing provided us with a sales script and it was incredible. It showed me the power of a good script that left nothing to chance. And the actual sales presentation was a sight to behold! **I learned the power of not one, but two incredible demonstrations** to show off the power of the product.

Real quick… these powerful demonstrations were:

1. Cutting a piece of bread in half lengthwise with a *super sharp knife* so it literally gave you two pieces of bread, each half a piece high. You must have a super sharp knife for this to work!

2. Cutting a piece of leather – but not a normal demonstration cutting; in this case, the prospect did the cutting. The customer didn't even have to saw back and forth. All the prospect did was push down on the leather and the knife sliced through it like the leather was not even there!

Those were powerful, powerful demonstrations.

Let me spell out for you the quick, valuable lesson that I got out of learning this sales process. **When you're selling, not only do you want to make interesting and exciting demonstrations, but you also** *don't want* **to reinvent the wheel.** Instead you want to model other people, systems and success templates – techniques that have been proven to work! There's a saying that "success leaves clues" and it's very true. So *don't* reinvent the wheel.

Another friend of mine, Andy Jenkins, aka "The Video Boss" says it a different way. He says, "Innovation sucks." Same message, just happens a bit more direct and memorable.

At the time, I used a burgundy hard-sided briefcase for all of my Cutco knives and my sales book – something I don't have anymore, but I still have my full set of knives two decades later and they work like the day I first received them.

Take 23 minutes…

…and **write a script you could use to sell yourself.**

And don't tell me that you don't use scripts; as my friend Eric Lofholm says, we all use scripts every time we speak! Try using a pitch based on both features and benefits. Don't forget to give a reason for every benefit you list. And wrap it all up with a hard-to-resist offer that includes proof and a killer guarantee.

By the way, the hard burgundy briefcase was one of my dad's old briefcases. It had two gold locks on it. (You know the type – locks with the three-digit combination that you set once and then forget how to change.) This was a pretty fancy briefcase for a young entrepreneur, and I'm sure carrying it increased my confidence level.

But back to the point where Mr. Dale Podhajsky agreed to meet me: Funny how I remember a few other sales calls that summer, but none really stick in my mind as much as this one. Grabbing my burgundy briefcase, I headed over to his house. I was driving my first car at the time, a silver Ford Probe that I bought from my parents – a wonderful little, fun car. When I got to the Podhajskys' house, I remember we met downstairs. It was one of those half-basements, half-outside downstairs that you see a lot of in the Midwest.

A short time later, we were going through my presentation; and I was feeling very confident. By the time we met, I had already done a few presentations, so I was getting really good at the demonstration. I had the script memorized, had all of my props – and I was getting very skilled at getting the prospect involved in the process.

Mr. Podhajsky was showing all of the classic buying signals. Very engaged, very interested – didn't ask how much longer it would take or if we were done. Didn't have a pressing appointment coming up. Yep, I really thought I had a live one here.

Then the time came for me to do my little closing pitch on him; and he said, "Henry, I'm not going to buy a set of knives from you today." My heart immediately sank, because I had been so sure he was interested. Then he said something very strange. "But, I'm going to do something even better for you today."

OK, I was honestly thinking that he was going to be buying two or three sets of knives instead of just one set. (That's me, ever the optimist.) Instead Mr. Podhajsky left the room for a few minutes.

I was left there contemplating and thinking. Running the numbers in my head and calculating commissions on the fly. You get really good at that, by the way, if you're working on 100% commission.

"OK, if he buys three sets of the biggest package, that means $2,400; at my 10%, that means $240 to me – plus I move up into the next tier and get a bonus of 10%, which means $480; and if I'm here for one hour, that means I'm making a *lot* on an hourly basis…

even after taxes. What will I do with all of that money? I really like that new computer game...!"

So he came back and not with his checkbook. *But he was carrying a book.* It was an old, tattered, and highlighted book that he gingerly set down on the table. I could immediately tell that he felt strongly about the book by the way he handled it as he began to tell me the story.

"Henry, I'm going to give you something much better today than if I bought a set of knives from you. I'm going to let you take a look at this book here." He gently picked up the book and handed it to me and said slowly, "This book is called *The Magic of Thinking Big* by David Schwartz. This book changed my life." I smiled politely and started leafing through the book with sunken heart.

By now the back of my mind was saying to me, "OK Henry, now get out of here; because he's definitely *not* buying three sets of steak knives."

The book looked old. It had a lot of highlighting and writing in it and the pages were getting brown. But skimming through it as he told me how it had impacted him in a big way, I started to feel a slight twinge of interest stir deep inside of me.

It was like he had ignited a fire deep down inside of me that began to warm me up from the inside out. See, up to this point anything educational I had read was for school. And any reading at home was solely for fun. Reading in school was because I was told to do it; I never read just for the sake of learning.

My mom was a big reader, but she was a novel fan. I don't remember my dad ever doing a lot of reading at home. He really enjoyed working with his hands on the weekends when I saw him most. He was, and still is, one of those amazing people who can fix anything.

Since I had graduated from high school a few weeks before, I had just this one last summer of freedom before heading off to college; so sitting around reading wasn't really my idea of a fun time no matter how compelling the book looked. But, for the first time ever, this book sounded *interesting* to me... no, more that that, it *fascinated* me.

See, it was the book itself that was tempting me. Standing there all on its own and begging me to read it and learn the wisdom it contained.

On that fateful day, the kindling of my mind was literally sparked to life by a very kind and successful man who decided to share a special book with me. **He may have seen something inside of me that I didn't see.** He may have shown the book to anyone who came to his house and gave him a sales pitch. He may have been in a good mood. I'm not really sure what motivated Mr. Podhajsky, but I do know that he chose to help me out that day and that our meeting has had a far and long-reaching impact on my life.

During our meeting this spark inside of me grew into a small flicker. I asked my host if I could borrow his book. I hadn't yet developed the habit that I have today. Now, I always buy my books so that I can make them my own.

Now when I read a book...

I highlight the book.

I write in the book.

I fold back the corner of pages I want to refer to later. (Dog-ear, I have learned, is the proper term for this.)

I will double-dog-ear the key pages in the book where I want to pull out actions by folding back both the top corner and the bottom corner of a page.

From especially good books, I will type up summaries and put them on my computer and on my smart phone.

BOOKS ARE TOOLS. THEY SHOW WEAR WHEN THEY'VE BEEN USED WELL FOR A LONG TIME.

Mr. Podhajsky agreed to let me borrow his book but only if I promised to return it to him in a week or two. I wholeheartedly agreed that I would. Then I spent the next few days going through that book.

Those few days were literally life changing!

THE WISDOM LEFT BY OTHERS CAN CHANGE YOUR LIFE.

That's why you're reading this book, after all.

I think Tim Ferriss said it best in his book *The 4-Hour Workweek*, when he recommended *The Magic of Thinking Big* and said, "The main message is, don't overestimate others and underestimate yourself. I still read the first two chapters of this book whenever doubt creeps in."

The Magic of Thinking Big talks about your thinking and how thinking controls your life. I had never thought about that, and the book was a real eye-opener for me. I finished it in just a couple of days and liked it enough that after I finished it I gave the copy back with a very big and hearty thank-you, and then went to a bookstore to get my own copy.

I still have my copy. Nowadays, it looks a lot like the one I held over twenty years ago. It looks old and used. It has a kind of smell to it that books get over time. I personally love that smell.

My copy has highlighting in it. It has notes in it. This is a book I've read several times. **Books are tools. They show wear when they've been used well for a long time.** Whenever I read a book a second or third time, I try to use a different color pen or highlighter so I can see what I thought was important on earlier readings and then mark down anything new that I find important this time around. *The Magic of Thinking Big* has seen me through tough times, has helped me believe in myself, and has helped me become the person I am today.

The first two chapters are my favorites as well as Tim Ferriss' favorites. Chapter One is "Believe You Can Succeed and You Will." It's a very mind-freeing concept to realize that literally all you need to do is believe and you can achieve. It's the same premise that Napoleon Hill was getting at in his now-famous book, *Think and Grow Rich* – still one of the best titles of any book, anytime, ever.

Take 10 minutes...

And **list three books you think everybody should read**. (OK, make it four books since the Bible should be on that list too.) Then add a sentence after each book title explaining why it's so useful.

I didn't just read that first chapter. I really internalized the message that it was sending. It was empowering to realize I could literally use my mind as my greatest asset. This was a completely novel concept to me, and I was very grateful to have found this wonderful book explaining it to me right there in black and white.

YOUR REWARDS ARE DIRECTLY RELATED TO HOW MUCH RESPONSIBILITY YOU TAKE.

And the second chapter spoke about how to "Cure Yourself of Excuse-itis, the Failure Disease." I thought I was pretty good at this; but hey, we all have work to do, don't we? This chapter helped me realize that I needed to stop making excuses for myself. This came full circle just a short time ago when I was reading an article by my marketing mentor, Dan Kennedy, in which he spoke about taking responsibility. The gist of his message was that **your rewards are directly related to how much responsibility you take.**

And a big part of that is eliminating excuses. Being rich and making excuses do not go together.

So really, the big lesson for me that summer was that I figured out I could literally tap into trillions of dollars of expertise and thousands of years of experience just by opening a book. Today I am a ravenous reader. In fact, when my two girls get older and start to do more of their own activities, I will transition to even more reading. Sure, I'll probably play more golf than my current one game a year quota, too; but it's having the time for more reading that is very exciting for me.

I've been amazed at how much reading I have done since that time. Most of my reading has been business, marketing and real estate books. I also like books on tape. Just yesterday I received four books in the mail. Today, one book arrived. Already, I've completely filled up my closet and my office. I look forward in the future to having my own personal library and study where I can keep all of my books.

And, now you're reading *my* first book.

As I continue to become more successful and be around more successful people, I realize that they all share something in common. They are all constantly learning more and improving their skills. And most of them are voracious readers. I had thought that once you left college, you got a job and basically were able to cruise from there on out. It's actually what I was doing myself until my eyes were opened from the "P" Lesson.

BEING RICH AND MAKING EXCUSES DO NOT GO TOGETHER.

If you only do the status quo, then you end up in middle management in some cubicle farm, doling out your 40-55 hours a week for a salary that barely sustains you – until someday you become part of a corporate downsizing in an action decided upon thousands of miles away by people that are completely unaware of the contributions you have made to the company.

THE CHANGE IN ME WAS IGNITED BY THAT BOOK RECOMMENDATION SO MANY YEARS AGO.

Not my exact story there, but I did experience one downsizing that did come from more than 5,000 miles away and was not related to the job I was doing at the time. That experience, I told myself, would definitely be my last downsize; and afterward I began the steps that would help me avoid becoming a permanent member of the rat race.

How did I escape? **The change in me was ignited by that book recommendation so many years ago.** As they say, we're always most grateful to those who show us the light of opportunity when we're stumbling around in the dark. I've been very fortunate to have many of these people who helped me on this journey.

At last count, I've invested more than $95,000 in books and my own personal education. This is NOT including the $50,000 or so that I spent on my college education.

The money I've spent on my own personal education has been the best investment I could ever have made. I hope understanding the importance of continual learning will inspire you in the same way it has me and that you also will invest in yourself and reap the positive benefits of doing so.

To get a list of my favorite books and home-study programs, please visit:

www.HourADayBook.com/resources

Here's your pocket summary of what we talked about here:

- Take time to improve yourself every day.
- We never progress in a straight line.
- You get out of something what you put into it.
- Don't reinvent the wheel when you're selling.
- Wisdom left by others can change your life.
- Eliminate excuses - Being rich and making excuses do not go together.

Your "Hour-a-Day Blueprint Tip"

So how do you get started in making the best investment... an investment in yourself in only an hour a day?

The fastest and easiest way is to convert your commuting and driving times into learning times. Get books on tape and invest in resources that have audio CDs or MP3s so you can plug into them while you're in your car. The best part of this is that when you listen in your car, not only do you actively hear what's being said, you will also be in an immersive environment.

Even if you work from home, try this anyway. I have a home office and an office five minutes away and I'm still able to get through a CD or two a week.

CHAPTER 3

TEN EXTRA SECONDS OF WISDOM:

Arguably the most important business
and wealth-building skill is marketing –
spend time each day learning more about marketing from
the masters and then implementing what you learn.
This is blue-collar work – just get your hands dirty by
taking action and seeing what happens!

IT'S ALL ABOUT
THE MARKETING

I attended and spoke at an event recently with several other successful entrepreneurs presenting. One of them talked in detail about the skills that have allowed him to become a multimillionaire in a very short time. Funny how none of the skills had anything to do with hard-core technical competency; instead nearly all of them related to one very important big topic… and that topic was sales, but more specifically, *marketing*.

SELLING AND MARKETING
ARE NOT THE SAME THINGS

Let me tell you a story from the late, world-famous copywriter Gary Halbert that illustrates some of the importance of marketing.

Gary was asking a seminar group that had come to learn about sales, marketing and copywriting about how he could win if they opened up competing hamburger stands, "What do you think is the most important thing you need to have with your hamburger stand?"

Answers flowed out from the room – answers that included "secret sauce," "the tastiest hamburger," "the best french fries," "a big-name franchise on the sign," and on and on.

Then Gary flatly told them that even with all of those things, he could beat everyone. He said that everything else didn't matter and that he would have the one thing that really did matter.

The room started screaming out other ideas.

But nobody got it right.

Gary then told them the answer to a successful hamburger stand: "The only thing I need to beat all of you with my hamburger stand is ... a starving crowd."

Selling is what you do once you get the crowd there. Marketing is how you get the crowd there in the first place.

This really is what marketing is all about.

> "Ideas are a dime a dozen, but the men and women
> who implement them are priceless."
> – Mary Kay Ash

It's critical for you to understand that it doesn't matter how good your sales pitches are or how great your marketing or advertising is if you're trying to sell something to somebody who doesn't need what you have.

SELL TO A STARVING CROWD

Let me share an example with you. The town where I grew up was very close to Buffalo, New York. In case you don't know, Buffalo is known as the snow capital of the United States. If I opened a surfboard shop in Buffalo with the best marketing, best advertising, best quality surfboards, rock-bottom prices, and every other advantage you can think of, it would be a tremendous failure.

The reason? Because nobody is surfing in western New York!

Of course, arguments could be made that you could take your business online; but shipping surfboards isn't cheap and local talent may be hard to come by; and so, for the purpose of this example, your business would fail.

Take a similar example in my current hometown, San Diego. I could open up the best snow blower and sled store for hundreds of miles around, stocking the best snow blowers, the finest snow shovels, the fastest sleds and toboggans, the best salt and sand, and the best ice scrapers, and I would have very limited success because it doesn't snow in San Diego.

> "Any idiot can make soap. It takes a genius to sell it."
> **– attributed to James Gamble,**
> **a cofounder of Proctor & Gamble,**
> **on the importance of sales and marketing systems.**

I learned this lesson at a very early age. My very first job was working for the world's most famous investor, Warren Buffet. Well, actually it was selling the *Buffalo Evening News* door-to-door in the mid-1980s and yes, Mr. Buffet owned that paper and still owns it today. As I look back now, I understand it was one of the easier things to sell for one very important reason. When I was selling the newspaper, people still read the newspaper! There were no competing newspapers in our area, and the *Buffalo Evening News* was very reasonably priced.

SELLING IS WHAT YOU DO ONCE YOU GET THE CROWD THERE. MARKETING IS HOW YOU GET THE CROWD THERE IN THE FIRST PLACE.

Therefore I was selling in a "competitive vacuum," which means no real competition. And I was selling to a hungry crowd. Those two factors by themselves made it relatively easy to have about 75% of all the houses in our neighborhood on my subscription list.

If I had to go back today and sell newspapers, with the advent of the iPad, the internet and smart phones, it would be much, much tougher to sell… at any price point.

One of my mentors worked many years for Copley Newspapers, which recently finished selling off all of its assets and closing its doors. The company shut down, but not because it did a poor job of running the business. It was actually known as one of the best-run and well-managed newspaper companies in the country;

but it closed because the market has completely changed and people aren't as "hungry" for newspapers any more.

There no longer is a starving crowd of newspaper readers.

So how does this relate to marketing?

THE MARKETING TRIANGLE

My marketing mentor, Dan Kennedy, talks about the marketing triangle; and I'd like to introduce you to that concept. I firmly believe that when a marketing problem arises, no matter how complicated it may be, you can always go back to the basic three sides of the marketing triangle to get your answer.

One of my favorite coaches was the great football genius Vince Lombardi, who began every season with a lecture to both the veterans and the rookies on the basics of football. He literally held up a football and said, "This is a football." He talked about its size and shape, how it can be kicked, carried or passed. Then he took the team out onto the field and said, "This is a football field." He walked them around, describing the dimensions, the shape, the rules, and how the game is played. He did that every year, even after the Green Bay Packers were NFL champs and won the first two Super Bowls ever played.

Can you imagine how basic and fundamental that must have sounded to his veteran players? And yet, maybe that explains why Vince Lombardi was such a successful coach; he began with the basics and was famous for focusing on the core fundamentals in his coaching.

The same exact thing applies here when it comes to sales and marketing. And to be successful, you can bring all marketing back to the marketing triangle.

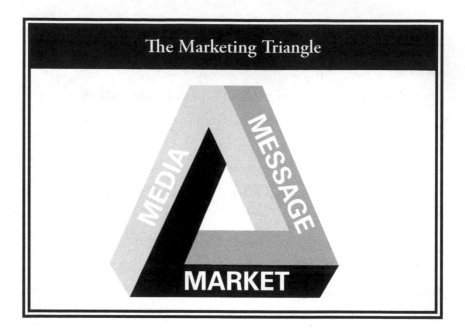

The first side of the marketing triangle is what we've been talking about already – the market. This is finding a market that wants to hear from you and has a hunger for whatever goods or services you are selling. Selling surfboards is easy if you live in a beach community in San Diego because the demand is high and people have a built-in desire for your product.

FIND A STARVING MARKET AND FEED THEM WHAT THEY WANT

I always say it's better to *find a market first* instead of coming up with a product first. Most people have it backwards; but in reality, it's far easier to find a starving market and then give them what they want. This makes your life as an entrepreneur much, much simpler than if you begin with a product and then try to find a way to sell it or to force consumption.

Most advertising and marketing is unfocused and not targeted at a prospective client. **When you transition to targeted marketing, aimed and engineered exactly for whom you want as your customer or client, your results will be dramatic.**

One of the biggest discoveries I've found in how to make money is that you need to *connect only with your ideal prospect.* You want to connect with those who have a strong interest in what you are selling. Realizing and acting on this is a game changer.

If we go back to our snow store example – this time with the store in Buffalo – even a poorly written advertisement or sales letter, exactly matched to the needs, desires, and problems of a targeted group of people experiencing a blizzard, can get great results. This is true the same way that an expertly written advertisement or sales letter, offering something to people with no interest in it, will fail.

THE SECOND SIDE OF THE TRIANGLE – YOUR *MESSAGE*

Quite simply your message is what you are communicating to your market. You have three different choices when it comes to your message. You can send no message, the wrong message, or the right message. Let's talk about each one of these in order.

Most advertising and marketing efforts really have no messages at all. They are what are known as business card websites, or business card advertisements. The reason we say "no message" is because they lack differentiation and a reason to respond *now.* Basically it just has the core information about the business and that's it. Open up any Yellow Pages or go online and take a look at most websites for local businesses in your area and you'll see exactly what I'm referring to.

There are also wrong messages. The worst are the ones that are exactly the same as everybody else's and are promising the best price or the best service. I especially dislike the ones that focus strictly on the product or service instead of where the focus needs to be – on the customers and their needs, desires and interests.

The worst reason to be advertising is desperation to find customers. The best reason is having something new, exciting, bold, interesting and different in an ad that it is designed to produce a response. The key thing to understand here is that **you need to have a USP (unique selling proposition)** that separates you from everybody else.

THE KEY TO YOUR MESSAGE IS YOUR USP

Dan Kennedy asks this question, "Why should I, your prospective customer/client/patient, choose to do business with you versus any and every other option available to me?" Note that he's not just referring to competitors, but to every other option. I've added a very important item on the end of this question: "including doing absolutely nothing." So, not only why should I chose you over any and every option, but also why should I chose you over just sitting on my duff and doing nothing? And for some markets, such as weight loss, that is especially relevant, since most will take no action at all.

Imagine this scenario: You're selling burglar alarms. You're really not selling against other competitive products most of the time; *you're selling against a person not doing anything at all.* Your USP needs to answer this exact question in the prospect's mind and give him or her a reason to choose to do business with you.

I taught an entire sold-out workshop on the subject of creating a compelling USP. It sounds easy in principle; but really, it's quite difficult to get a good core message that resonates with your audience and differentiates you from your competition. The most famous example is from Domino's; its USP was "Fresh, hot pizza delivered in 30 minutes or less, guaranteed, or it's free."

Take 30 minutes...

...and **design a USP.**

Realize that it does not have to be perfect. Actually, most USPs change over time. Make two columns. In the left-hand column, list the last 10 things you bought at a grocery store. Just grab a receipt, or do it from memory. And just generics, not brands. So "shampoo," not "Fiji Tea-shake Balsamic Mushroom Hair Soap."

In the right-hand column, brainstorm 10 USP statements that answer the question, "Why choose you"?

Now the real twist: Avoid superlatives. No "best" or "fastest" or "biggest."

The result will be a list of 10 authentic USP statements. Doing this on other products or services unrelated to your own will help you when you brainstorm your own USP.

After many strategy sessions, one client that I'm working with right now was able to engineer his USP to get at the core result his prospective clients really want. He sells to salespeople and sales managers and his message was originally a non-USP, not unique and not selling him at all.

When we were done, his USP became *"Catapult your sales 30% or more… Guaranteed or it's free."* This captured exactly what his target audience was looking for. They didn't really care about anything except getting results.

THE SECRET TO A GREAT USP IS THAT IT IS FOCUSED ON YOUR CUSTOMER OR CLIENT, NOT ON YOU OR YOUR BUSINESS. IT'S BELIEVABLE AND AUTHENTIC.

My client has actually helped a lot of people achieve 100%, 200% and even 300% growth rates; but that might seem a little unbelievable to a new prospect, so we toned it down just a little bit into 30% or more catapulting of sales—and the market is responding very positively.

The secret to a great USP is that it is focused on your customer or client, not on you or your business. It's believable and authentic.

If you're interested in going through my USP workshop, where we have detailed questions and exercises to help you get your own USP, please visit:

www.HourADayBook.com/usp

Unique selling propositions are rarely stagnant; they get adjusted, tweaked and modified over time. The idea here is to practice the process of continual improvement. The earlier example I gave of the newspaper company going out of business might be attributed to the fact that those who ran it thought of themselves as being in the *newspaper business*, instead of thinking of themselves as being in the *media or knowledge business*.

One of my favorite classic examples is those in the railroad industry thinking of themselves as in the railroad business. Most of them went bankrupt. Instead, they should have realized that they were in the *transportation business*. If they had figured this out and adjusted their USPs, then we might be flying on Union Pacific Airways today.

UNDERSTAND AND APPLY DIRECT RESPONSE OFFERS

The second biggest "message issue" you need to understand and apply is direct response offers. The ideal process in most marketing is to establish a system in which your ideal prospective customer or client raises their hand and identifies themself by requesting a widget. Widgets are valuable pieces of information that your target market wants, like free information, free reports, free audios or free videos offering a powerful benefit.

They request these from you and thus begin to take baby steps in moving toward becoming a customer, and that allows you follow up with them effectively. Anytime you see an offer on TV or in print offering you a free CD to get more information, you're seeing this kind of effective "lead generation advertising" in process.

What happens, after you get permission and get the lead, is that you can put in place an effective, multistep, multimedia follow-up sequence to develop a new customer. The good news is this strategy works both online and off-line; and being able to create new widgets or well-crafted irresistible offers is a very important skill that's critical in developing a good message that resonates with your target.

MEDIA TO GET YOUR MESSAGE TO YOUR MARKET

Let's pull it all together and discuss media. There really aren't any good or bad media. Media are simply a distribution tool: They are a way to get your message to your target market. There is no shortage of variety here. You can use online strategies, or off-line media such as radio, television, direct mail or magazine ads. There are literally dozens of ways to get your message in front of your target market. The key here is to choose media that your target market is currently paying attention to.

One example of marketing that really illustrates this is a Lexus dealership that is sponsoring the valet service at a high-end shopping mall. People who have their cars parked by the valet service receive a small booklet advertisement and an offer from this Lexus dealer; and if you happen to drive a Lexus your valet parking is free. This is just another form of media, in this case sponsorship advertising, getting the message and offer from this Lexus dealer into the hands of the target market, which is wealthy patrons frequenting this high-end mall.

Take 28 minutes…

…and **write a perfect classified ad.**

Make it fit in a box three inches wide and five inches in height, like an index card. In fact, use an index card!

Look back at the USP you created a few minutes ago. Can the USP be expressed in an image? Is there a way to use fewer words for your USP?

Remember, **don't re-invent the wheel here.** Look at other classified ads in your target media so you can see the offers that they are using. If you see an ad over and over again, that usually means it is working and is worthy of study.

Now take the card to a friend or family member and get his or her reaction to your ad. Then, run your ad to see how well it works – there is no substitute for live testing in the marketplace.

One of the biggest things to learn here is not to limit yourself to just one medium. Most businesses rely on one, two, or maybe three different types of media. Imagine the power and flexibility and profits you can obtain if you have *10, 15 or 20 forms of media* all working profitably on your behalf. The competitive advantages are enormous because your competition will continue to just use a handful, while you are able to get business in many other ways. The Lexus dealer above is a great example of this, because it is the only sponsor of the valet parking at this high-end mall, and thus is reaching people that no other Lexus dealer will be reaching, let alone other luxury car dealers that only advertise in traditional media.

Now that you have seen why you need to learn how to use *all three* sides of the marketing triangle – *Market, Message and Media* – to get good results from your marketing, there is one last thing that I'd like to point out. As you learn and discover marketing strategies to propel you and your business forward, don't let yourself get in the habit of thinking your business is different from all others or that these marketing strategies won't work for you.

USE ALL THREE SIDES OF THE MARKETING TRIANGLE TO SOLVE ANY MARKETING CHALLENGE

These strategies will work for any business – yours included!

I know of them being used in thousands of different businesses, have personally seen and helped implement them in more than 100 businesses, and I've used them in five different businesses of my own. Whether you are selling to businesses, consumers, end-users, or the government, they work and work well.

So here is an important thing to realize, and it can unlock an untold amount of riches when you do: You, as a smart entrepreneur deserving of maximum profit, are able to see successful marketing and advertising from any type business—even from a success-ful plumber—and **find something you can use in your unrelated business.**

This "translate and transfer whatever works" mind-set is a very valuable personal asset. You can develop it over time by hanging around smart marketers. And if you need to know how that's done, just see Appendix A at the end of this book and you'll find that a Mastermind group is a great place to meet smart marketers to hang around with!

Here's your pocket summary of what we talked about here:

- Marketing is how you get a crowd to contact you.
- Selling is what you do once you get the crowd there.
- Sell to a starving crowd and focus on the market, not the product.
- Remember all three sides of the marketing triangle – message, market and media.

Your "Hour-a-Day Blueprint Tip"

So how do you get started learning the most valuable business skill of marketing in only an hour a day?

I recommend that you commit to at least 30 minutes a day reading and studying direct response marketing books, tapes and CDs. This is something that takes time to absorb so the faster you get started, the better the results you are going to receive. The secret is to read, listen and study this daily – this ensures the maximum retention for you.

Secondly, I recommend that you spend the other 30 minutes a day writing out successful ads and copy in long hand and discovering the most profitable skill of copywriting. There are incredible resources available that you can begin to follow today. I give you all of the details on the best and newest ones when you visit:

www.HourADayBook.com/copy

CHAPTER 4

TEN EXTRA SECONDS OF WISDOM:

I try to never finish up a day
without doing something to grow my list –
your relationship with your prospects and customers is
critical so spend some time each day making your list
larger through some proactive activity.

YOUR

MOST IMPORTANT

BUSINESS ASSETS

B efore we go into this chapter about your second most important business asset, you need to understand what is your first most important business asset. And it might not be what you think.

The truth is, **you are your own most important asset.** The skills, expertise and experience you build for yourself are what are most vital to your business or businesses. Always make sure you are taking primo care of your best asset, yourself.

So, with that in mind, let's go ahead and talk about the second most important business asset. We're not talking about customers. They *are* the business. We're talking about something much more strategic.

I've been involved in businesses for more than 20 years, but I didn't learn this lesson until recently; and as I look back at my successes and failures, I know for certain that I could have shortened my learning curve and gotten wealthy a heck of a lot faster had I understood and applied the principle I'm about to reveal to you. This is something profound but simple; but whatever you do, don't underestimate its power when applied to your business.

It doesn't matter at what phase in your business you find yourself today… this applies to *you*. It doesn't matter what business you are in – if you have customers, clients or patients or want to have customers, clients or patients, then this applies to *you*.

And here it is:

The Second Most Important Asset of Your Business is Knowing and Understanding the Importance of YOUR LISTS.

I'm sure you must be wondering what "lists" could possibly be so important. What lists are we talking about here?

The lists we are referring to are your own developed lists. The creation of your lists, their maintenance and use, and their continual growth are the most important things you can do to add real, lasting value and equity to your business.

"There is only one boss. The customer. And he can fire everybody in the company from the chairman on down, simply by spending his money somewhere else."
– **Sam Walton, founder of Wal-Mart**

There's something a lot of people miss, so I want to clarify it before we go onward by answering this question: Which lists do you need to maintain and keep?

MOST PEOPLE DON'T JUST COME IN AND BUY SOMETHING. THEY RESEARCH IT FIRST.

Everyone immediately thinks about their *customer* list when asked if they have a list. Let me relate a funny story about this list.

Recently, I was doing a complete marketing overhaul for a successful local dentist who said he had a very large list. As it turned out it was much smaller list than I would have liked, but it was a good list. However, it was a list of only his *current customers* and that was the only list he had. He had nearly 700 customers on his list, but he didn't have any other lists.

So I asked him, "How about all of the people that have made inquiries over the past two years? Where did all of those leads go?"

He told me, "We didn't keep those people; they didn't want to work with us so we threw them out."

Uh oh, this wasn't good. Let me explain.

Think about yourself in regard to this. **Do you always go into a store and buy the very first time? Of course not**; usually it takes between five to seven contacts to make a purchase (even more when buying online). This applies to everything from cars bought at a dealership to baby strollers bought online.

On average, according to extensive studies, 5% of purchases are done during the first contact. But 95% of purchases take longer and take multiple contacts.

Now, please don't start saying that your business is different, because *it isn't*. It doesn't matter what business you're in. The fact is that **most people don't just come in and buy something. They research it first**, they go browsing, perhaps phone in for more information. Now, if you sell gasoline at the corner store, you might be in the 5% of purchases that are done during the first contact. However, the vast majority of purchases take longer and usually involve multiple contacts.

So, let's agree that 95% of purchasers do not buy a product immediately, but need some time to think it over. Then it becomes critical that you follow up with those prospects, so when they are ready to make a purchase they gravitate toward you and your product or service.

IT IS ABSOLUTELY IMPERATIVE THAT YOU *FOLLOW UP WITH PROSPECTS* AND STAY IN FRONT OF THEM.

So, that means that you need to have a list of *prospects* for follow-up. First, let's define "prospect" to clear up any confusion. What exactly is a prospect? It's a member of the 95% that contacted you but didn't buy right away. It's someone who, metaphorically, has raised his or her hand to express interest but has not yet purchased.

OK, so what do you do to turn that prospect into a customer? Most businesses do little or nothing. Think about the stack of business cards that you have next to your desk... that's exactly what I'm talking about. Good intentions to follow up but no reliable follow-through.

The most important thing right off the bat is that **you need to capture that prospect's contact information during that initial contact** so you have the opportunity to follow up.

One of the very first things I did when overhauling the marketing of my dentist client was ensure that he had a lead-capture system in place, so that he could collect all of the people that had an interest in his product or service but might not have signed up right away. This involved having a lead-capture offer on his website and offering an incentive to those calling in on the phone to give their name, email and address.

Realize that you need to offer something of real value. Getting signed up for your email newsletter doesn't work any more. Think about what your ideal customer would absolutely want to have – what they *must have*. What knowledge do they need, what video would they want to watch?

Take 5 minutes...

Flip through a few channels on TV to find a lead capture offer. One of my favorites is TemperPedic Mattresses, which doesn't just sell you a mattress right away in the ad. Instead, it offers you a free DVD so you can learn all about the benefits of having a great night's sleep, free of back pain.

How do you create your own lead-capture offer that is irresistible?

Then, you add all of these prospects to a prospect database *every single day.* It's important to capture as much information as you can so you can follow up with them in multiple ways.

Next, you regularly and consistently stay in touch with them. This way, when they are finally ready to buy, you have been keeping in touch with them and you have "top of mind" awareness.

Guess what?

Say you own an auto repair shop and a prospect keeps hearing from you, month in and month out with a relevant and entertaining newsletter, even though all the while his car doesn't need fixing. What happens when his car doesn't start tomorrow morning? The guy who gets the call is the same guy who has been keeping in touch. Keeping in touch gets you the sale – and you get the new customer.

Now, there are many ways to stay in touch with your customers regularly, and keeping in touch doesn't mean that you're always sending advertisements or offers. In fact, it's often better to provide valuable information and become a resource and a credible authority to help them learn more about the problems that your product or service solves.

This can be done with an informative newsletter, email newsletters (also known as ezines), direct mail, promotions, educational materials, special reports, teleseminars, webinars...the opportunities are endless.

What you are doing is educating and building up a *relationship* with the prospect over an extended period of time so that when they are finally ready to buy that car or that baby stroller, they will contact you and give you the business.

This is an immensely powerful concept for you to understand. It's also a tremendous opportunity for you, because nearly all business owners underestimate the power of creating these lists and then following up... including your competitors.

Take five minutes...

...and learn a little about lists.

• **List five businesses** you think have you on their lists. How did you get there? Are you a customer of theirs or a prospect of theirs?

• **Name five individuals** or businesses you feel should be on your list of customers. Guess what? They will need to start as prospects so what could you offer them to entice them to become a prospect of yours?

• **Bonus example:** For my Marketing Summits, I advertise to local entrepreneurs and I have a free three-part video series called "Marketing Training Videos for Local Businesses." Many who end up becoming customers start by requesting this free, valuable information. This is a great example of a lead-generating system that works on autopilot.

So, you can see the power of having great lists – not only segmented by customers but also segmented by prospects. Having this in place is vitally important to your business.

Let me tell you how I've heard the value of the "list" system explained. It's like the difference between hunting and farming.

While hunting definitely has its place, it takes a lot of effort to go out and close new sales every single day, which would be like going out and hunting for dinner every single day. **With a lead-capture and follow-up system in place (farming), prospects are attracted to you** and see you as a valuable source of information. Then, as you educate them over time and build up a relationship by providing valuable content to them, you become the only logical choice in their minds for the product or service you offer. This means that you become a harvester, easily turning these warm leads into customers – *when the times comes that they are ready to buy.*

TAKE GREAT CARE OF YOUR
CUSTOMERS AND THEY'LL
TAKE GREAT CARE OF YOU!

To give you an example of this let's take my dentist friend. He pays for a service that writes a monthly newsletter for him. You could also write a newsletter yourself; but I've found it's usually easier to have somebody else do the bulk of the work for you, so it doesn't take away from other things you're doing.

WITH A LEAD-CAPTURE AND FOLLOW-UP SYSTEM IN PLACE (FARMING), PROSPECTS ARE ATTRACTED TO YOU

The dentist writes just one or two small articles in a four-page newsletter every single month. Most of the information is fun and entertaining, and there are also tips on oral hygiene and dentistry. He also has a small article focused on him and his family that is very important. It is a patient-centric newsletter, focused on the patient, not just talking about the dentist and his credentials.

As this newsletter is sent out over a period of time, people begin to have a virtual relationship with the dentist. They begin to feel as if they know him, and have an affinity toward hearing from this friend every single month. This relationship develops even if they aren't already a patient and have not even met the dentist.

An example of this kind of relationship is how you feel about celebrities. I remember seeing Jon Lovitz from *Saturday Night Live* fame at a famous diner near UCLA. I immediately felt an affinity for him, as if I knew him, and wanted to go up and say hello. Of course I had never actually met him, but **a virtual relationship whether through TV, video, print, or radio can have the same impact as a**

real relationship… especially in this day of YouTube, Facebook and Twitter. In fact, these are real relationships.

The lesson to be learned is that you want *to become a trusted friend and adviser* by building up a relationship with your list on a continual basis. You do this by growing the list and then providing valuable information and entertainment. And don't underestimate the value of entertainment. Those who just provide information in a dull fashion commit the #1 sin in marketing… being boring!

As you do this over time, you will start to get new business, leads and referrals from people who feel as though they know you, but who really have only a virtual relationship with you. One funny point on this is that a virtual relationship can often times be better than a real relationship. It's a lot harder to screw up a virtual relationship because you control the entire dialogue with your prospect!

NEARLY ALL OF THE WEALTH CREATED IN BUSINESS HAS ITS ROOT IN LISTS

Some people think that the assets of a business are the physical machines, the products or the services. However the real assets of a business are the lists of customers and leads and the relationship with those lists.

Since so much wealth comes from the lists, I want to give you a quick overview of mailing lists and mailing list basics. Part of the information below is courtesy of my marketing mentor, Dan Kennedy.

Studies by the U.S. Postal Service and companies in the mailing industry such as Pitney Bowes consistently show that 60% of small business owners rarely – if ever – use direct mail; but of the 40% who do, 90% say it is *the* most productive means of marketing they employ. This reveals how big a competitive advantage you can claim by becoming smart about using direct mail. Using direct-mail marketing requires getting smart about lists; in fact, lists (the "who" you mail to) are at least as important as what you mail or what you offer.

MAILING LIST BASICS

There are four kinds of lists and means of getting lists:

1. Your own customer or prospect lists. You *must* have, maintain and use a list of your present and past customers. No one is more likely to respond to you with a low-cost marketing approach than your own customers, and most business owners lose a great deal of money by not communicating frequently enough and presenting enough offers to them. And *every* effort should be made to move *every* prospect to your mailing list. Visitors to your store who don't buy; people who call and ask questions; people you meet socially – you need to get them all on your mailing list by whatever means possible.

2. Lists you compile yourself. Published directories, for example, often offer the opportunity to compile free mailing lists. Most national, state and local trade, business and professional associations have directories of their members. A B2B (business-to-business) marketer may be able to find prospects in the Yellow Pages, or by observing companies' advertising. Many businesses, groups and others list their customers or members on their websites. If you belong to a group, you probably have a directory of the other members. Think of this as "guerilla list-building" done "on the ground," sometimes surreptitiously. As a B2B (business to business) marketer myself, if I wanted to reach out to exceptionally progressive business owners these days, one of the things I'd do would be to take the Inc. 500 list of fast-growth, emerging midsize companies published annually, have each one Googled® to obtain complete info, then add as many as seem a fit for me to my prospect database – and probably send a special "congratulations" mailing as well.

3. List built through lead-generation advertising. I want to get to prospects when their interest begins, but before they buy. If I owned a local pet store or were a dog breeder, I might continually run a lead-generation ad like this:

> Before You Buy ANY Dog ANYWHERE,
> Get This FREE Special Report:
> "10 Smart Questions to Ask Before Choosing a Dog"
> and a FREE DVD:
> "Secrets of the Obedient, Well-Behaved Dog"
> Free Recorded Message, (000) 000-0000 or
> online: www.SmartDogOwner.com

4. Rent commercially available lists. Here's a crash course in list rental, in the form of a list:

- *Most lists are rented per use*, not bought for unlimited use.

- *Compiled lists are assembled from public information*, and typically involve (only) basic demographics or statistical information, with significant margin of error. Examples of compiled lists would be: married, age 30 to 50, with kids, homeowners (not renters), household incomes of $50,000 and up, in these zip codes...or (in B2B) companies with 10 to 50 employees, sales within a certain range, by SIC code, by zip code.

• *A local list broker* (found in the Yellow Pages or referred by a printer/mailing house) may be able to meet these needs for you. Good national sources are Info-USA and SalesGenie, accessible online.

• *Response lists* comprise buyers, subscribers or inquirers of certain companies, so you can get names of actual customers. For example, if you operate an upscale restaurant, you might want Gourmet or Wine Spectator Magazine subscribers in your area or American Express cardholders who frequently dine out. If you own a home furnishings store, you might find buyers from certain catalog companies valuable.

• *Renting* such lists is more complicated and costly; some companies won't rent to direct competitors, your mailing must usually be approved in advance, and there are usually 5,000-name minimums, which a local area may not provide (forcing rental of thousands you can't use to get those you want) – but all this can be well-worth the hassle and cost, as other means of obtaining names of known buyers perfectly matched with you require even more expense and time. To access these lists, you will need to consult, educate yourself with and shop SRDS, which stands for Standard Rate & Data Service, the master catalog of all commercially available response lists. Begin educating yourself by checking out www.SRDS.com. Another favorite of mine is www.NextMark.com, which is an online version of the SRDS service and is available for no charge.

• *Selects* is the term for the many ways many lists can be segmented or broken down: age, gender, marital status, home ownership, occupation, etc.; and in buyer lists, category of goods bought, price, frequency, etc. Typically, each select adds to the cost per 1,000.

• *Brokers, managers, compilers.* A company such as InfoUSA is a "monster compiler" of all sorts of consumer and B2B lists from public records, surveys and other sources. Most response lists of any size are placed by the companies that own them with list managers, who handle all the details of getting them listed in SRDS, advertised in marketing trade journals, cleaned and maintained, and delivered to those using them. Sometimes you'll deal directly with a manager, but usually not.

• *Brokers are commissioned middlemen who handle clients like you and secure lists for you.* Often brokers tend to specialize and represent many lists in a specific category (health; travel; financial), so they can be helpful in recommending lists. Each list's broker and/or manager is listed in SRDS with the list information itself. If you find one broker representing several lists that interest you, it may be easiest to form a relationship with that one broker.

• You should know in advance that no one is eager to do a lot of work with small-time operators who do not offer potential of renting entire lists after tests and of frequently renting lists. One way around this is to simply suffer the indignity of minimum service in order to get what you want. Another is to organize peers with businesses just like yours in different parts of the country to go together as one renter of a large number of names.

TRIPLE TIPS

1. Don't be intimidated and don't be lazy! It's worth the time and effort to become knowledgeable about lists. I can promise you that a few hours roaming through SRDS will open your eyes to targeted marketing opportunities to perfect customers for your business you never before knew existed!

2. Look for hidden costs. When considering list rental costs, don't forget to factor in all the other costs of finding exactly suited customers who are known buyers…or potential buyers who match up perfectly with your customers by other means, such as advertising.

3. Do your homework. The more you know about your customers, best customers and desired customers, the better you can find matches in available mailing lists.

Here's your pocket summary of what we talked about here:

- You are your most important business asset.
- Your second most important business asset is your list(s).
- Most people don't buy right away so make sure to follow-up with your prospects.

- Create great lead capture offers and put them into automated systems.

Your "Hour-a-Day Blueprint Tip"

Realizing the importance of your list and growing your list are paramount to business success. Your Hour-a-Day tip is to do at least one thing every single day to grow your list. If you take this action, you will start to see real list growth very quickly.

Let's get tactical for a minute – you must begin to harness the power of your lists, and begin collecting not only all of your customers' information but also all of your prospects' information so that you can follow up appropriately.

List-management systems change very quickly – companies come and go, some get worse, and some get better.

I have put together a full review covering the pros and cons of each system I recommend for list management. You can get a short and powerful walk-through of each so you can make an informed decision on how to select the best one for your business at the webpage below:

www.HourADayBook.com/lists

CHAPTER 5

TEN EXTRA SECONDS OF WISDOM:

When you spend time daily
on what's important in your business –
work to a countdown clock and get things done
as quickly as you can. Working to deadlines
like this will give you a tremendous
productivity boost!

THE SECRET OF SPEED

"MONEY LIKES SPEED"

When I hired my first website designer many years ago, he said something that really made an impression on me. While it was not super impactful at the time, I wrote down what he said because I had a feeling it was more important than I was crediting it with at the time.

We were working on a complete website overhaul for a very large, content-rich site. There was a lot of work to be done, and I had hired him personally for this project. He was the most expensive website designer I had ever worked with at the time ($150 an hour). Most website designers I had worked with cost half that or even less, but I had a good feeling about working with this guy for a couple of reasons. Reason #1 was that he really understood website design and website technology. And reason #2 was that he also really understood marketing.

I knew that he was the right person to assist me with this first website revision, so we went ahead and engaged to work together. In doing so, I was making a very large investment for a site that was bringing in so little money at the time.

We began the project, and everything was going quite smoothly. We had the usual back and forth as we worked on the new pages but nothing out of the ordinary. I had sent a deadline for getting the site completed very quickly. Essentially we were planning to get a 100-page website done from scratch in 21 days.

I was working on most of the content, creating and rewriting; and he was working on the pages themselves, hand-coding them in search-engine friendly html. (Now that I look back, I sure wish we had an easier platform we could have used to develop the website.)

Eventually, we were nearing completion of the project and probably had only three or four days of work left. He was operating fast and getting things done, and so was I – along with my partner at the time – getting edits, changes and responses right back over to him.

Then he made this comment to me:

"This is good Henry; you work fast and money likes speed."

> "The world is changing very fast. Big will not beat small anymore. It will be the fast beating the slow."
> – **Rupert Murdoch,**
> **media magnate, philanthropist, and founder,**
> **chairman, and CEO of News Corp.**

Now, he said this right in the middle of some other things that we were talking about regarding the site. But there it was, this comment that money likes speed. At the time, I didn't know or think that money really liked anything, let alone speed. I had never heard that before, but it impacted my consciousness to the point that I jotted it down in my notebook before going on with the business of finishing the website.

About a year later when things were taking off, I really began to understand how profound this comment really was. Why? Because, money really *does* like speed and is attracted to speed. It is completely impartial to how fast you want to earn it. Want to get money slowly? OK, then it will come very slowly to you. Want to attract money quickly? OK, that's what you'll get. Money really doesn't care at all which one you choose!

I've also heard the same philosophy stated this way: "There are certain steps that it takes to become a millionaire. You can do those steps in six months. Or six years. Or 60 years. Or never. But the steps remain the same."

But the faster you work and get the right things done, the faster money will be attracted to you and what you are doing. This relates to another story regarding speed. It's a fable you probably remember from childhood: Aesop's "The Tortoise and the Hare."

WHY AESOP NEVER MADE A MILLION

The story concerns a hare that ridicules a slow-moving tortoise and is challenged by him to a race. The hare soon leaves the tortoise behind; then, confident of winning, decides to take a nap midway through the course. When he awakes he finds that his competitor, crawling slowly but steadily, has beaten him to the finish line.

What does this have to do with speed you may be asking?

Well, funny you should be asking, because you would think you want to be the tortoise, right? Slow but steady and all that. Well, there is something to operating slowly and steadily – it's nice to make progress on a daily basis and to be always moving slowly ahead. But, **in real life,** *it's often the hare that wins*, because taking fast action, getting things done, and keeping things in motion are all critically important to achieving success.

I try to act like the hare in my daily actions – moving quickly as I complete projects. But working consistently and making progress daily, like the tortoise.

I love the Nike slogan, "Just Do It." It sums up what fast action is all about. I remember a very clear illustration of this principle in action.

I was talking to two people (one later became a client) about separate business ideas that they were working on. One of them actually had two tremendous ideas and the other one had one very good idea. They were both in the initial start-up phase but had done their initial legwork and research to ensure they had a good market to go after – which they both did.

This was an extremely important first step. When working on a business venture, it is important to always, always, *always* start with the market; never start with the product. Too many people fall in love with their product before even discovering whether there is a market for the product they want to sell.

So, friend number one, let's call him Tony – the one with two ideas – ended up starting his business with these two ideas at the same time.

My other friend, let's call her Jessica, ran with her idea and got that started.

Tony worked by taking action in spurts. He would get something done, then invest in a new program or get excited about something else, and then come back to the main project. His action was much more like the tortoise – slow, but gradually moving forward.

Jessica took a different road. She laser-beamed her focus and spent a lot of time quickly implementing every idea she could think of. She was like a hare – and sometimes even a little hare-brained: Jessica's website unfortunately was initially completed with a website designer who used an expensive and proprietary system that wouldn't allow her to even edit her own website without going through the designer.

Take 37 minutes...

...and **list what you can do yourself.**

When you start a new project, the temptation is to get everything out-of-the-box: hire help, buy software, use plug-in marketing solutions, template a retail site.

Often these things work best because they work quickly – right out of the box. And they work quickly because they bring an instant solution to a complex problem.

But the fastest way to get most simple things done is to do it the Nike way: Just do it. Get'er done. *Nail it.*

So before you start any new business or launch a new business project, **make a list of what you need to buy – and another of what you already have.** The stuff you already have is what you know how to do, and you can use that stuff without even waiting for the box to arrive.

So, one of the first things recommended to Jessica was to scratch this expensively developed site and move to an entirely new website platform called WordPress. So, in many respects, Jessica was weeks behind Tony at the beginning. An important side note here is that Jessica was open to this kind of coaching. I've made similar recommendations to others who continue to have issues with their websites because they didn't heed this advice.

But, that was only the beginning.

Because she was acting with purpose and speed, Jessica got more done in a 30-day period than Tony did in a 120-day period. Also, because of the speed and action, Jessica's venture is now magnetic to money and opportunity. Joint venture opportunities, upsell options, and partners are now coming out of the woodwork.

As I write this, Jessica now has a marketing funnel in place that is systematized to produce high-quality leads at a profitable investment, which means that for every $1 she puts into marketing, she's getting back $1.35 – or 35% profit. She just got her first book written and published. And she is producing more than 100 times the revenue that Tony is producing.

MONEY AND MOMENTUM

Tony, while making progress, is operating at about a quarter of Jessica's speed. But, it's not just that; because of the focus, speed and implementation Jessica gets something even more important – *momentum*.

Ever watch a basketball or football game on TV?

You can literally feel when the momentum shifts from one team to the other. And you'll hear the announcers comment on it. When a team scores four baskets or two touchdowns in a row, that team is likely to continue on that winning streak.

So now that Jessica's business is up and moving and profitably producing leads and customers, things are starting to snowball. She's been approached by a very, very big joint venture partner (with more than two million list subscribers). Jessica is starting to get mentioned in the press and getting opportunities to be on radio and TV. She is seeing more opportunities than she had even thought of before taking massive action.

One niche in particular is for a part of the marketplace that nobody foresaw but that can be an absolutely huge source of new clients for her. I strongly believe that if she were not taking massive action, she would have never seen this opportunity ... or it would have taken years for her to finally become aware of it.

All of this while Tony is still trying to get his marketing turned on so he can make more than the first four sales. Jessica has already received hundreds of sales, raised her price three times, and built up a list of more than 10,000. Tony's list just topped 100.

There is nothing wrong with slow and steady, but don't expect big opportunities to knock down your door if that's your method.

All because *money likes speed.* Remember that the next time you think about taking fast action on an opportunity or mulling it over and thinking it through.

Newton's law: "An object in motion tends to stay in motion, and an object at rest tends to stay at rest."

Henry's Twist on Newton: "An entrepreneur moving fast and making money tends to move faster and make even more money."

Jessica is obviously using that to her advantage and Tony obviously is not.

The best part is that this is a choice that you make every single day.

Do you want to move quickly today and make things happen, or do you want to move slowly today and wait for things to happen to you? I heard a great expression that brings this down to a level that we can all understand – so let's go back to the common language of sports and say that you are playing basketball.

Let's agree that there are two primary modes of play during a basketball game: We can be playing offense – trying to score – or we can be playing defense – trying to keep the other team from scoring.

When you're moving slowly, you end up on your heels playing defense. This is the way of the tortoise, always worried about who might be looking to hurt him and then going completely defensive by hiding in his shell.

Moving quickly is more like playing offense. You're looking to score and take fast action against your opponent. This is the way of the hare because he is always looking to take fast and decisive action and quickly "hopping" to make things happen.

Can you win a basketball game by playing defense 100% of the time?

Of course not. You will never score any points playing that way.

All the same, you can't play offense all of the time either. But remember, the object of most games is to **score the most points.**

So it just goes to show that those who are successful spend more time on offense – taking fast action – than they do on defense. This is a common thread among winners. While others are busy planning what they're going to do and the great business they're going to have, the real winners have already called their attorney, bought a domain name, started assembling a team, put a marketing plan in place, and are making it happen.

TUNING IN TO GREAT ADVICE

There's a great CD I listened to several years ago that was all about taking fast action and getting things done. The person being interviewed had several successful businesses already moving and told a story of being out of town at a seminar.

While on this trip, he had one very important goal that he was looking to achieve. He was delivering real estate seminars, and his current radio advertisements had started falling off their response rates. Since he didn't know what was going on, he went to this event looking for a specific answer.

Because he went to the event with a specific goal, he found a great idea on how to tweak his radio advertisements that had fallen off with their response rates. His ultimate goal was to change his radio ads so he could generate more leads.

Now, what would the vast majority of people do after given this information on exactly what to do?

1. They would then proceed to finish the rest of their trip (four days).

2. Upon getting home, they would go through their email, run errands, read regular mail and water their plants (two days more). Then (if they were especially diligent) they would finally get around to looking at their notes from the trip and upon seeing that great idea, they would then put it on their to-do list (two days more).
Just so we're clear, we're already 10 days post hearing the initial idea.

3. There it would sit on the to-do list until they finally got around to it. Let's assume this is a faster breed of tortoise and this takes them only a week.

4. *Now* they are ready to either record a new ad or book an appointment at a studio. Let's assume this is more of a perfectionist tortoise who wants to book studio time.

5. Because the studio is a busy place, it takes seven days before they get into the studio with their preferred sound engineer.

6. Once there, they record the new ad and then send it for editing.

7. The editor usually takes a week or two, so now they wait for him. Of course, they want it to be perfect, so they go through a few revisions with the editor and this ends up taking even longer. Let's conservatively say 10 days.

8. Finally, the ad is sent to the station to be played and they work it in the next day.

TIME FROM IDEA TO THE NEW AD PLAYING ONLINE: THIRTY-FOUR DAYS FOR THE TORTOISE.

And I challenge you to take a look at any idea that you have thought about doing and see if you don't follow a similar pattern of slow progression with soft deadlines that often leads to poor results.

If you can't relate to this, that is good news! Because realize that no matter where you are today, there is always room for improvement. I'm constantly on the lookout for ways I can improve my speed of execution as well.

Now let's look at what my friend did.

1. He heard the idea while at the seminar.

2. That afternoon in his hotel room while on the break he scripted out his new ad copy to record (it wasn't perfect, but it was good enough).

3. He then got out the Yellow Pages and looked up studios in St. Louis, where he was at the time (not a perfect location, but good enough).

4. He had to call several but found someone who was happy to take his money and record the ad the next morning (probably not the best studio, but good enough).

5. The next morning he was in the studio and recorded his new ads very early in the day before the seminar started (the recording wasn't perfect, but it was good enough).

6. Immediately after recording, he had the new ads emailed to the radio station with no formal editing (no music, no fancy stuff, just him reading the copy… again, good enough).

7. He ordered the radio station to begin playing the new ad that afternoon. (Why not? It was good enough).

And, guess what, his new ad was playing that very afternoon in place of the old ads.

Time from idea to the new ad playing on-air: 24 hours for the hare.

Remember the time between the idea and it being fully implemented for the tortoise? It was 816 hours.

So when you look at things this way, the tortoise wasn't just a little slower than the hare. The hare was a *full 34 times faster* in getting the project completed than the tortoise!

Now, was the end result of the hare as good as the tortoise's?

No.

Did it sound as nice as the tortoise's ad?

No.

But it was done 34 days sooner than the tortoise's. And, since he acted fast, it was literally worth tens of thousands of extra dollars in the pocket of the hare! And, now my friend could adjust his ad and run multiple tests before the tortoise even unpacked his suitcase.

> "Eliminate the time between the idea and the act, and your dreams will become realities."
> – Dr. Edward L. Kramer

I love the saying that a good idea acted upon is 100% better than a great idea not acted upon. This is the same rule of life in play above. Marketing and business is a matter of taking swift action. Those who do so will reap much larger rewards.

Every fable has a moral. Here's the moral for this one: Be the hare, not the tortoise.

THIS IS A TEST OF YOUR MARKETING SYSTEM

That's the real answer to every marketing question.

I can't tell you how many times people will ask me a specific marketing question. "Hey Henry, do you think this postcard will work better than this one? What if I change the picture or headline here?"

Or "Henry, what do you think about this landing page that's getting a 20% opt-in rate? How can we make it better? Should we use video? That always works better, right?"

While I give ideas and best practices to clients, here's the evasive, yet true, answer that I add on every case: "I'm happy to give you some ideas, but here's the real answer. Marketing is easy: All you need to do is test, test, and then test some more."

See, that's a huge secret to marketing. **All that you really need to do is test out your ideas in the real world, with real prospects, to see what works and what doesn't work.**

Let's talk about an example – we'll make it a landing page on a website. What is a landing page? This is the first page someone who sees an advertisement goes to when they visit your website. You never want them going to your home page; you want them going to a specific landing page so response rates can be tracked.

The purpose of the landing page is usually very straightforward – get people to sign up (or opt in) on your list or get them to trade their contact information for something useful that you're going to give them, usually something you give them for free. For example, if going to a dental website, it might be, "Enter your email and I'll send you my Consumer's Guide to Selecting THE BEST DENTIST absolutely free."

As mentioned before, the vast majority of people do not purchase when first visiting a website. In fact, it usually takes eight to twelve "touches" before someone feels comfortable enough to make a purchase.

So, with that idea in mind, the smart marketer decides to generate a list of interested prospects first, then, via a follow-up system, convert them into a buyer at a later time.

Now, there are a *lot* of different ideas on what works and what doesn't work. You will find a lot of people today saying, "Video on landing pages is the only way to go."

Well, now, is it really? That's like saying that a Ferrari is always the faster car regardless of whom you're racing. But what if you are pitting a NASCAR racecar against a 1930 Ferrari Scuderia? Of course, you'll win.

What if we flatten the Ferrari's tires and put sugar in the gas tank? Then you'll even be able to win riding on a bicycle.

So the question is loaded from the get-go on what works and what doesn't work in marketing. The real answer is that there are best practices that may or may not work well for any given situation. But, the ultimate solution is to *test* out whatever you think may or may not work.

And, importantly, what works today may very well *not* work tomorrow, so you need to be in a continual state of testing, modifying and tweaking what you're doing in your business.

Let's talk about video on landing pages again. I'm involved in a successful online business that sells a training program primarily to high school basketball referees. We thought that video would be just amazing to increase our opt-in rates. But, being astute marketers, we tested this out instead of just changing the site.

Take 45 minutes…

…and **hire Google to do your work for free!**

You may be surprised to find that online testing can be done with a free service provided by Google called the Google Website Optimizer. Google has tons of free training on how to run these tests, but the simplest (and usually the best kind of test for most getting started) is a split test or an A/B test. This just means that when people visit your site, 50% of them view one page, and 50% view another page.

• The system takes care of measuring the results for you – and making sure that everyone who visits is served up a different page. And, if a visitor comes back to your site, it will be the same page when they revisit.

• After you get a statistically significant number of visitors, you can start to draw some conclusions. Again, the software automatically tells you exactly how this works and what percentage chance you have of winning if you choose one page over another.

You don't need to do this personally – its better handled by your webmaster, but it's a good thing to understand at least the mechanical basics.

So, using Google (see box) we tested a video vs. a non-video page. And, believe it or not, the video page *lost* to the non-video page.

What this means is that more than 4% fewer people opted for our free giveaway when we used video on the page! We tried several different videos and finally found one that tested about the same, but even then, on this particular website with this particular audience at this particular time, video lost to text.

Now, the curious among us will start to ask, "Why is that?" Well, my hypothesis was that these prospects were probably on slower computers, or might not have speakers on their computer, and therefore weren't able to experience the video as it should be seen.

However, we then tested audio on the page to see if playing audio only could beat the text. And, it did test better than the text!

So, why is that? Nobody really knows why. But, the right answer is, "Who really cares?"

If you tested and found out that a picture of you riding around on a bull with a big No B.S. sign over your head tested higher than anything else you did and made you more money, then you'd probably spend a lot more time riding around on bulls, right?

Coincidentally, that's what my marketing mentor, Dan Kennedy, has as his logo – him riding a bull with a big No B.S. above it. Not because he wants people to laugh at him but because it *actually tests higher* than any other image he has tried.

So, if you are ever in doubt on what to do or how to do it or if someone questions you about marketing or business, if at all possible just **set up a test and that will lead you to the answer.**

More often than not, you will not be able to guess what your prospects will or will not choose. I've put together amazing advertisements that follow every single rule of direct-response marketing and they were beat out by something completely different.

THE BOTTOM LINE IS THAT YOU NEVER KNOW UNTIL YOU TEST

And, these tests can be done offline as well as online. Usually offline they are done via coupon control.

For example, say that you run a veterinary hospital and you want to test out two offers for new residents moving into the area by sending them a postcard. One offer is to give them a free healthy-dog examination and the other offer is to offer them 20% off their first visit.

Which one will work better?

To determine the answer, take a list of people you want to send the offer to and then randomly split the list in two. The direct-mail piece should be virtually identical except for the offer. In fact, the less you can change, the more you'll be sure that your change is what's producing the difference in response.

So, in this case you send 2,000 postcards with the free offer and 2,000 postcards with the 20% off. The cards are identical except for the headline and the offer: same kind of postcard, same fonts, same pictures, etc. (A golden rule of testing for beginners is to test only one thing at a time.)

Let's say that you get 50 responses on the free offer and 10 responses on the 20% offer. Guess what, you now know which one of these two offers the people or businesses on your lists like better.

The next thing to do is make the free offer your "control piece," which means it is the current, reigning champion, and now it's your job to test against it until you can best it. So here, you might want to test a 50% offer against the free offer to see how well that does.

TEST AND TEST YOUR WAY TO SUCCESS

As you continue to do this, your marketing gets better and better over time as you test and test your way to success.

Like most marketing, it all ends up coming down to mathematics, how much you are spending and then how much you are receiving in return.

The most experienced business people literally view their business as a laboratory for constant testing and improvement. They are running experiments all of the time to squeeze out a few more percentage points here or there to earn more opt ins, get some more leads, and sell more products and services.

You, too, should do the same with your business. **Don't believe opinions! Test things for yourself.**

Here's your pocket summary of what we talked about here:

- Take fast action.
- Don't be the tortoise, be the hare.
- Money likes speed.
- Testing is the key to successful marketing.
- For beginners, test only one thing at a time.
- You never know until you test.

Your "Hour-a-Day Blueprint Tip"

Your Hour-a-Day Blueprint tip is to spend a few minutes seeing exactly how a real split test works. I've had a screen video recorded to show you exactly how to do split testing quickly and easily. Look for it here:

www.HourADayBook.com/test

CHAPTER 6

TEN EXTRA SECONDS OF WISDOM:

Spend 15 minutes of each day planning out
what you're going to be doing the rest of the day –
your top goals and your affirmations. You'll see at least
a 2:1 return on this time invested.

YOUR LIFE:

IT'S ABOUT TIME

L et's talk about time management. There's more to time management than you might think; it's actually life management that we're talking about, because when you really look at time you will realize, "Time is life."

YOU TRADE YOUR LIFE, OR YOUR TIME, EVERY SINGLE DAY BY WHAT YOU CHOOSE TO DO AND WHAT YOU CHOOSE NOT TO DO

Let's delve into some of my most valuable time strategies, and some areas where you may have gotten stuck and how to overcome these roadblocks.

Time management is a real passion of mine, and I want to walk you through some strategies I've discovered that have enabled me to get a lot of things done very quickly. These are specific strategies I've learned and used that I have gotten from a variety of sources through the years.

My interest in time management goes back to before I was 10 years old. My father always had a Day-Timer planner, and I believe I had my first one in the late '70s before I was even 9 years old. Of course, this came from wanting to be like Dad and have the same kind of cool things that he had. I just saw him recently; he's retired on a 43-foot trawler with Mom, traveling the Great American Loop. Funny thing is, he told me the best part about being retired is not having a Day-Timer any more!

As I look back on some of those old planners, I can see that I already was beginning to understand how important time was, although I didn't yet realize that my time really was my life. Even back in college I took a Franklin Quest seminar (Franklin Quest evolved into Franklin Covey, still a leading provider of time-management services) with my then-girlfriend – for some reason she wasn't nearly as interested in it as I. My library has dozens of books on time management and I've studied this subject for a very long time.

I've also come to realize and appreciate the value of journaling. I've done this for many, many years, although not nearly as consistently as I would like. The real benefit I found in spending the time to put your thoughts on paper every day is that it makes your thoughts more real and concrete. Doing it with goals is doubly powerful; goals become much more achievable when committed to paper.

The ideas I'm presenting to you are cafeteria-style. Pick and choose what works for you and what doesn't. I'm also going to make recommendations on some other resources you should investigate;

and then you can create your own customized plan that works best for you, your goals and your needs.

> "Dost thou love life? Then do not squander time,
> for that's the stuff life is made of."
> – Benjamin Franklin,
> *Poor Richard's Almanac*, June 1746
> author, diplomat, inventor, physicist,
> politician, and printer (1706-1790)

FOCUSED TIME BLOCKING (GUILT FREE)

Before I go into the details of how I recommend doing time blocking, it's important to cover an area most people have issues with. And that is the idea of guilt if they are not "on call" all the time to clients, customers, patients, family and friends. It's now a familiar analogy, but I liken this to playing defense versus playing offense. If you do nothing but play defense, or be at the beck and call of everybody else, then you really set yourself up to be in a reactionary position all the time.

All of these activities cause your productivity to go down dramatically:

- Checking your email throughout the day.
- Driving your car and checking email or texting on your smart phone (this can also shorten your life considerably).
- Getting text messages from people throughout the day.
- Taking inbound phone calls and checking voicemails.

The only way I've found to become really productive is to *block my time* so that I can focus 100% on the task at hand. Understand that I only started doing this recently; the guilt I experienced at first was tremendous.

I guess my feelings about it not only were driven by guilt, but also had a lot to do with my addiction to constantly being needed by others. We all have an urgency addiction to one extent or another. Breaking through this was really important for me to begin to see benefits from time blocking without continually worrying about what I was missing.

Take less than five minutes…

…and **make a time-priority list.**

List the things that take the most time in your day and work down to the thing you give least time to. Now compare this list to the list you made at the beginning of this book – the one that asked you to list the things that matter most to you.

Which things recur on the lists? What do they reveal about the way you invest time? (And if this takes you more than five minutes, that tells you something, too.)

The other thing that's really important is to be present with whatever it is you're doing. Constantly being interrupted immediately lowers your mind's effectiveness, because you're not able to be truly present with what you're doing at that time.

Let me give you a great example of this. As I was writing this book, I knew that it was a project that should have been done within a very short time frame because it's all about topics I know really well and nothing is too complicated or difficult. However, I was not time blocking and therefore wasn't making progress on this book as quickly as I knew I should.

The slow progress was because *I wasn't focusing*. I would write a page or two and then be off checking email or answering a phone call or researching online, which would lead into a 20-minute internet tangent. You get the idea. After I purposely focused and blocked time to work on this project, I've now been able to get most of this book done within a few days.

I found the best way to be guilt-free when you're doing time blocking and focusing is to just set the expectations with others. One of my Mastermind Members, Christine McDannell of Social Starfish, takes this to the extreme and actually doesn't check email two days a week, on Tuesdays and Thursdays. So the footer on every one of her emails says, "I'm not checking email on Tuesday or Thursday and I thank you for helping me escape email jail!"

I FOUND THE BEST WAY TO BE GUILT-FREE WHEN YOU'RE DOING TIME BLOCKING AND FOCUSING IS TO JUST SET THE EXPECTATIONS WITH OTHERS.

While you don't have to go as far as Christine does, you do need to set the expectation that responding to email does not have to be done instantaneously; and you need to explain to others how often you communicate and how you use email and not let email use you.

Once you are in a guilt-free state, you will be able to fully focus on blocking your time. Let me explain why this works so well.

WHY TIME BLOCKING WORKS

The gist of time blocking is that you put all of your energy into **doing exactly one thing for a fixed amount of time.** As an example, I set up this two-hour block I'm in right now just to work on this book. That means I won't be checking my email, answering the phone, or allowing myself to be interrupted in any way. Short of someone breaking an arm, or experiencing an event such as an earthquake, people I work with know that I am not to be disturbed during this block of time.

That degree of focus may be impossible for you to do with your current environment. That means that you need to get out of that environment and get into a new one... as quickly as possible!

COMPUTERS AND TIME

Laptops are a great tool for environment problems because you can take work out of the office and go someplace where you will not be interrupted. This can be an office that you rent, it can be the beach, or it can even be at the library. I've used all of the above, and just getting out of my environment almost always helps me be more productive.

I also recommend that you have **a single computer for keeping all your information and that this primary machine be a laptop.** That way, you never have the excuse that you left that file here or there on your other computer. I've made the mistake of trying to have multiple computers, and this is one thing you want to avoid. Even though I now have four PCs, I have one primary laptop – a new Macbook Pro 15, which is easily the best laptop I've ever owned. And

I use a great, free cloud-based service called DropBox.com to keep my files in sync on multiple machines.

Speaking of what to invest in, I've used both PCs and Macs. I was a late convert to a Mac and switched over in early 2011. It was a good move, because after getting through the learning curve, I'm able to get more done on the Mac faster and easier than I could with the PC. Video is especially easy now on the Mac. It took a couple of months to learn all of the shortcuts, but it was worth it for me.

Bottom line is, whatever works for you is fine, but put everything on your laptop and in your DropBox so you always have everything ready and with you, wherever you might be. A nice benefit of using the Dropbox.com service is that it automatically backs up your data as well. Want to discover my top 5 online resources that I use daily? Visit www.HourADayBook.com/freevideos.

WHEN TIME BLOCKING, MAKE CONCRETE APPOINTMENTS WITH YOURSELF

It's critically important that time blocking is valued as much as an appointment you would have with a big client, especially if things are urgently in need of getting done. If you have an urgent task, it becomes even more important that you block your time and stick to your schedule. One thing that's been very difficult for me is estimating how long a given task will take. Learning how to estimate time needed is something that comes only with practice. Until then, set blocks of at least one hour and don't be afraid to set time blocks of four hours each or even up to an entire day or multiple days.

Another thing that I didn't realize until I started blocking my time was that **I wasted a lot of time changing gears on multiple projects.** I sincerely believed that I had to work on a lot of things each day to be successful and productive. This is not the case at all, and this thought pattern held me back for years.

There are days now when I have just one or two activities time blocked. This is very hard for most people, as they then feel they are letting a lot of other balls drop while they are focusing on just one activity.

Take 19 minutes...

...to **see how your time is really organized...**
...or disorganized.

At the end of today, take an unused day-planning page out of your pocket calendar or print one from your computer.

Disregard what your own calendar says you did today, and instead **reconstruct your day** on the day-planning page.

If you have more than two or three discrepancies, your time today was poorly organized.

Further analysis: How many discrepancies were the result of unplanned events? How many were the result of misappropriation of time for specific tasks?

Time is money. If you don't really know how you're spending it, you'll have a very tough time getting wealthy.

If that's you, reread the section above on guilt. You need to be guilt-free when you block your time. Don't be afraid to block two, four, six, eight or even 12 hours straight to get a project finished. Don't make the mistake of trying to time block large projects in 30-minute increments, because it may take you years to get done.

I'M FIRMLY CONVINCED THAT A ONE-HOUR BLOCK OF UNINTERRUPTED, FOCUSED TIME IS WORTH MORE THAN A FULL DAY OF CONTINUOUSLY INTERRUPTED NON-PRODUCTIVITY.

When I started, my entire business grew in one-hour time blocks per day. That's where my success – and the genesis for this book's title – came from. **I'm firmly convinced that a one-hour block of uninterrupted, focused time is worth more than a full day of continuously interrupted non-productivity.**

The momentum that you get as you start working on a project you've time blocked is tremendous. It's something that you have to experience to appreciate. When you schedule and go through a four-hour time block for a project with no distractions, then you will start getting substantially more done than you normally do.

I recommend taking a break every 50 minutes and taking 10 minutes to stretch, walk, or even do a few push-ups. The important thing here is that you do not engage on another project or check email; you just disconnect and let your mind wander a bit. Nothing works better than a quick walk around the block to get the blood flowing and get the mind cleared so that you come back re-energized and reinvigorated. If you do look at another project, that can quickly turn into a 15- or 30-minute rabbit hole of lost productivity, so don't tempt yourself.

As you begin to time block, you'll find that your efficiency goes up dramatically; but this may mean that at the end of the day you have only one thing to check off on your list. This was a really big problem for me at first.

How could I say that I was productive if I got only one thing done?

Are you anticipating having that feeling right now?

That's OK if you are. It's very normal to feel a lack of accomplishment when you have accomplished only one thing in a day. However, as you begin to see the results of actually completing projects, you will quickly realize that getting one thing done in a day is much better than spinning your wheels on a dozen different projects and not making substantial progress on any of them.

Don't think of checkboxes on your list as a measure of success; it is about the quality of what you get done. Getting one good project or task done in a day is something to be proud of and something that fortunes can be, and have been, built with.

One last comment on time blocking, and that is on scripting your day.

PLAN OUT YOUR DAY JUST LIKE A MOVIE SCRIPT

Some very successful people actually plan every minute of their day. You certainly should carefully use every minute of the day, because each is extremely valuable. I don't feel it's necessary for me to script every minute, but if that works for you then by all means go for it. The bottom line is that you must be focused and you must dedicate 100% of your energies to exactly what you're doing at the moment in time that you are doing it – and keep pushing until you get it done.

I usually recommend scripting and planning 75% of your day – especially your morning, to work on high-impact, high-return projects, i.e. those that will create income and wealth for you. Then, leave some time in the afternoon for email, follow-up, and those miscellaneous projects that always seem to come up. For example, my car is now flashing a low-tire-pressure light. I don't want to schedule an appointment with the garage, but it needs to be done. And, better it gets done at 5 p.m., when I'm winding down the day, than at 9 a.m. during my prime-time work hours.

WORKING TO THE CLOCK (PRODUCTIVE BEFORE A VACATION)

You know how you're able to get so much work done on the day before you go on vacation? I've asked this question to rooms filled with hundreds of people I was speaking to, and nearly everyone can relate to this. What's the reason behind that sudden burst of productivity?

I believe the answer is that when we're working on a countdown, when we know what we need to get done and we know the time frame we have for getting it done, it almost always gets done. If this works so well right before a vacation, why not use it every single day to dramatically increase productivity and take vacations more often?

Take 15 minutes...

...and schedule your own stay-cation.

If you're anything like me, you enjoy a good vacation. Even a stay-cation is a fun diversion from normal day-to-day living. So, plan a two-day vacation with yourself to get an important project done. Go out of town and stay at a hotel. Tell your family you have an important business trip.

Doing this will allow you to completely unplug from your normal routine and get a lot of work done in a short amount of time.

I actually have two friends that have each done this and each gotten their books done in 48 hours during their stay-cation. Give it a go.

That's exactly what I discovered with my technique of working to the clock.

The first thing you need here is a countdown timer. If you have an iPhone or iPod Touch, that will work great. You'll find a great one inside the clock application called the timer feature. I use multiple countdown timers. I have a kitchen countdown timer from Taylor.

It's inexpensive and works great. You can pick one of these up at any discount store. I also now have a very fancy, remote-controlled LED timer on my wall – it looks amazing and is huge! (If you want a tour of this, I'll show you all of my clocks and timers if you visit www. HourADayBook.com/clocks.)

You need to use what's best for you, but the idea is that you **give yourself an amount of time to get a job done, and you hold yourself to task** to do whatever it takes to get the job done in that time frame.

As mentioned above, I really like working in 50- to 100-minute blocks. I find I get restless after 100 minutes, and sometimes I need to get up more often, so I'll set my countdown timer for 50 minutes. On a typical day for me, there will be four hours blocked in the morning for a project, I will work 50 minutes on, 10 minutes off for each of those four hours, and then stop for a quick lunch.

There are a lot of valuable tips in this book but **if the only thing you take away from these pages is to purchase a countdown timer for yourself and use it, I guarantee you'll be both impressed and astounded with the results.**

THE DAILY LIST

One of my favorite business mentors is Brian Tracy. I was fortunate enough to spend a day with Brian Tracy and Mike Koenigs filming a product launch that I was orchestrating. We spent lots of time in between shoots talking, and over lunch we chatted about family and what it takes to succeed in today's business climate. It was a phenomenal experience and one that I will never forget.

One of the things that sticks out in my mind is something Brian Tracy said when we were talking about our kids going to school.

His kids also went to a Montessori school, and he was very happy with how it taught them to be self-sufficient. He also said **the most valuable thing that you can do is to teach your kids to be entrepreneurs because nothing will better ensure their success in the future,** regardless of the job climate and what happens with our government.

To fully appreciate this next part of the story you have to realize that for many years I have found different quotations and words of wisdom from thought leaders like Brian Tracy and added them to my quote list. Before we met with Brian Tracy, I looked at all of the different quotes that I had from him and especially reviewed the first one.

EVERY MORNING GET UP AND WRITE OUT ALL YOUR GOALS FOR THE DAY.

I'm sure it was no coincidence that when we met he actually pointed to the same quotation I had long ago carefully recorded as words of wisdom to live by. I view this as the most valuable thing I've learned from Mr. Tracy, and it has dramatically helped me to be successful. So here it is...

Success guru Brian Tracy was once asked what one single thing he would teach his son if he could only teach him one thing. He responded by pulling out a sheet of yellow paper and said, "If I could only teach my son one thing it would be this – **every morning get up and write out all your goals for the day** and carry it with you throughout the day, focusing on one goal at a time. At the end of the day throw it away and do it again the next morning."

This is **the power of having a daily list.**

Take four minutes right now...

... and **make a daily list** for yourself.

What are your top priorities to get done today? Goals come from your vision and plan that you have for your life. Everything boils down to the present moment and today so what are you going to do to move you one step closer to your goals?

Always start with the daily list.

So the question becomes, "What exactly do I need to do today and what are my goals for today?" If these daily goals are always kept on top of your mind, they will have a dramatic impact on your life because each day will become **a focused effort toward achieving exactly what's most important to you.**

So when you invest in your countdown timer for $10, also pick up a $2 yellow legal pad and you'll have all you need to practice the idea of the daily list as well as time management.

If you want to get a little fancier, you may want something akin to the moleskin diary book that I have and try to write in every single day – or for the digitally focused among us, get yourself a Livescribe. com pen so everything you write is digitally recorded.

GTD PHILOSOPHY

I owe a debt of gratitude to David Allen for writing the book called *Getting Things Done, The Art of Stress-Free Productivity.* I can't do the book justice by talking about it briefly here, so I highly recommend that you pick up a copy; or if you happen to already have a copy, go dust it off and reread it. This book has some phenomenal lessons on personal productivity.

I'd like to share with you two of the major concepts that made a big difference in my life and how you can use them immediately in your own life.

The first concept is that of operating from a zero basis. This means that if your mind is clogged with lots of things that you need to do or think you have to do, it makes it very difficult for you to focus on exactly what you're doing and where you are right now.

David Allen's solution for this is to make sure you operate with a mind like water. This means you write down and get every single open-ended loop out of your mind and put it into a trusted system. This is best illustrated with a quick example.

NO OPEN LOOPS – THE KEY TO HAVING A MIND LIKE WATER

Let's say that I'm driving to a friend's house and I notice my car is pulling to the left. Upon getting to her home, I notice that my front left tire is low. When I get back home I put some air in the tire and make a mental note that I need to get the tire looked at when I have some time. However this is not put into a trusted system; it's not written down; it is a "mental only" note to myself. This means I just created an open loop in my mind.

As I'm driving a week later I notice again that the car is pulling to the left and mentally remind myself that I need to get that tire checked out. But I don't get it checked and so it remains an open loop in my mind, taking up valuable mental processing for a trivial task that I shouldn't be actively thinking about.

Because I don't have a trusted system yet to record this low-priority task, it never gets done and continues to worry me until I get a flat tire as I'm driving home late one night in the dark. Then I get mad at myself for not having gotten the tire fixed a lot sooner, and now I have no choice but to get it fixed right then and there in the middle of the night, causing me aggravation and grief.

So what is the answer for this kind of conundrum?

It's actually quite simple. **Every single idea you have, task you need to accomplish, or project you're working on needs to go into a trusted system.** That way you don't have to actively think about anything other than what you're currently doing. You don't have to remember to get your spouse an anniversary present because that's already been put into your trusted system, and you know that the reminder will pop up on the appropriate day and you will then order or plan something for him or her.

Along the same line, let's say that you have a mechanic friend who can work on your car, so you call him and schedule an appointment for Thursday. The reminder is then placed into your calendar, and your mind can rest easy knowing that the problem will be solved soon.

The fundamental cause of stress is failure to place tasks like these into a trusted system but instead keeping these types of things in your mind as open loops. Every open loop that you have in your mind creates a small amount of stress and doesn't allow your brain to rest. Your brain knows you will forget things if it doesn't constantly remind you.

Once you have a trusted system put in place, your brain is able to truly relax, because it knows that you are not going to forget; the system will do the reminding for you. It is magical when you get a system like this put into place, because you will be able to be truly present with everything that you do at all times, rarely if ever getting stressed out or worried about things you should be doing but may have forgotten about.

RELAX...
IT'S ALL IN YOUR
TRUSTED SYSTEM

THE WEEKLY REVIEW TO MAINTAIN YOUR SANITY

One of the other key things that I've learned from David Allen's book is the idea of a weekly review. Allen calls this a critical success factor, which means that all of your open loops, or projects, are reviewed once a week. This gives you an opportunity to make sure that your brain is clear and that all of the loose ends of the past few days have been collected, processed, and organized into your trusted system.

This is what puts everything together and what makes sure that the little reminder about your tire that goes into your inbox gets processed Friday afternoon. Since it is a very small task, you get it done immediately by making an appointment for the following Thursday. The weekly review is the glue that holds the entire system together and allows you to operate in a state of relaxed productivity.

There are a lot of other things that I do and follow from David Allen's book, but these two have had the greatest impact on my own personal effectiveness, and I'm very grateful that I made the small investment for this book that truly changed my level of productivity.

Don't forget that every day and every minute you are living in the present moment and making choices about where and how you choose to spend your time. **Make sure to choose wisely.**

Here's your pocket summary of what we talked about here:

- Time management is life management.
- Perform focused time blocking (guilt free).
- Get my top 5 online resources I use daily at www.HourADayBook.com/freevideos
- Make concrete appointments with yourself.
- Plan your day like you're going on vacation the next day.
- Have no open loops - put everything you do or need to do in a trusted system.

Your "Hour-a-Day Blueprint Tip"

Want to get the most from each hour and wondering what technology the most successful people use? Check out the page below, where I will give you an overview of the technology I use on a daily basis to get the most work done quickly.

www.HourADayBook.com/freevideos

CHAPTER 7

TEN EXTRA SECONDS OF WISDOM:

Spend time in gratitude each day for what God has
blessed you with. And give away good every day –
whether it be a smile, some money or just a kind word –
this all comes back tenfold.

TWO ULTIMATE BONUSES

There are two bonuses that I want to share with you. First, I want to share something with you that has made a big impact on me and a big impact on others that I know who have also used it.

It is the idea that the hole that we give through is the same size as the hole we receive through. We reap what we sow, and the more we give the more we receive.

WE REAP WHAT WE SOW

This is another of the lessons that didn't sink in for me until recently, but I have now realized how important it is to give back to others and to help others. This is not only for the reason that it makes you and those you are helping feel good, although it does do that.

Another very important reason for giving, however, is that what you do unto others will come back to you many times over.

I love the story of John D. Rockefeller walking around handing pennies to people in the streets. If you've read anything about Rockefeller you know that there was a reason he did this: He knew it would all come back to him; and I'm sure you'd have to agree that he was right, and everything he gave came back to him and then some.

So how do you use this lesson for yourself?

You make sure to give to others as you would want them to give to you. This doesn't always mean money. It can mean giving time, talent, resources, introductions, or just a helping hand. By giving of yourself, your money, your resources or whatever you have to offer, you will make others feel better, you will feel better yourself, and it will end up helping your bank account as well.

As an example, I just shared a plan with a friend via email on a proven marketing program to find a new job. He's not an entrepreneur and has no interest in being an entrepreneur, but we put together a marketing plan for him to get his dream job. Normally I would charge at least $5,000 for designing such a program, but because he is a friend, I did it for free with no expectations of anything in return. If and when I do receive anything in return, it will be a nice bonus, rather than an expected result.

Another way to say the same thing is what goes around comes around. One of my favorite personal examples of this axiom is from an early job in which I learned my $10,000 lesson.

Someone I was working for very early in my career promised me I would receive a bonus after working for him and his partner a few months after I started. This bonus would have been equal to about $10,000 over a year. Now, put that in the context that I was making only $18,000 a year at the time, and you can see that this was a substantial amount of money, a nearly 50% bonus on my annual income!

When the time came to get my bonus, the person I was working for conveniently forgot the deal we had made. I realized he had never intended to pay me anyway and learned a truly painful lesson from the experience.

> "The antidote to frustration is a calm faith, not in your own cleverness, or in hard toil, but in God's guidance."
> – Norman Vincent Peale

Later, I ended up working for somebody else in the same office. When my previous boss didn't have me available to help close a large transaction, he lost out on a commission that would have netted him a quarter of a million dollars.

That kind of makes that $10,000 seem small, doesn't it?

What goes around comes around. But don't take my word on this one– just try it yourself and watch what you distribute come back with increase.

In a more positive example, I decided recently to make a donation to the YMCA. My two daughters and I are members of the Indian Princesses tribe within the local YMCA. You may have heard of Indian Guides; I participated as a kid with my dad. This is the same group – Indian Guides is for dads and sons, Indian Princesses is for dads and daughters who get together for camping trips and fun events each month.

The YMCA was doing its annual fund raising, and our goal was to be the top group in participation and in dollars raised. Times were tough for some in our group, and I wanted to help. The recommended donation was $100 per dad. I decided to give $500 instead. And, one of our dads ran our donations through his company, which matched our contribution, making my donation worth $1,000.

Now, most would say that this was very generous. Please keep in mind that I didn't expect anything in return and was happy to do it, but something did come back, and very quickly indeed. In fact, within 24 hours of making that donation, an unexpected check appeared in the amount of $2,200. Was that a coincidence? Think what you will, but **I firmly believe that what you send out comes back and in bigger amounts**. Try it yourself and see what happens – just remember that when you give, do so with the expectation of nothing in return. Let me know what happens to you when you try this.

Your "Hour-a-Day Blueprint Tip"

Give something each and every day. Whether it be a smile, some words of encouragement, some money, some time, some attention. Give something. And give without the expectation of receiving anything in return. This can make a big difference for you in your life and will impact you tremendously if you try it.

THERE IS A GREATER PURPOSE FOR ALL OF US

One very important last thing that has made a tremendous impact on my life is having *faith*. This is related to the flow of energy and the metaphysical as well; but I call all of that faith. The benefit of faith does not depend upon whether you believe in God, Buddha, Mohammed, or another religious figure; but Jesus is whom I believe in and I really believe He is God's son and that He is *the* light in this sometimes dark world of ours.

Regardless of your religion or absence of religion, the fact of the matter is that none of us are here on this earth for more than a short time. Time goes quickly and I'm sure you've seen as you've gotten older that this becomes more and more apparent. Friends change, buildings change, kids change and grow up, our bodies change also; and nothing seems to stop the relentless marching of Father Time.

Take 17 minutes…

…and **be still.**

Do this every day at the same time: sit up straight, shoulders down, chin slightly lowered. Set that countdown timer of yours for 17 minutes.

Focus on your breathing; if necessary, use a word or phrase to regulate your breath so it's steady. If you're spiritually inclined, think of God. I also like to visualize breathing in clean white energy and expelling the negative, grey and black energy. Close your eyes, but don't doze. **Be still** until the timer goes off.

It was a very happy day when I met my future wife many years ago. One of the many gifts that she has given me is her strong faith and the fact that she attends church regularly. I grew up in the Episcopal religion, but my family did not attend church very much. As I got older, my attendance became less and less until it was a once-a-year happening during Christmas. I really didn't know the meaning of Easter until much later in life. Imagine my surprise when I realized that Easter was actually a bigger holiday for us Christians than Christmas!

Deep inside of me I began to realize that there was some greater power that was controlling everything that happened. This is what really gave me the faith and the courage to leave the corporate rat race.

Without that faith, I would not have been able to make the jump. I think that's why I had worked in the rat race all of those years before meeting my wife. I was just too scared to go out on my own. **Once I found her and I found my faith, I experienced the belief that I would be taken care of regardless of what happened to me with any job.**

There was a lot of yelling and screaming inside of myself when I made this change. All of my fears, my doubts, all of my past programming, all of my schooling – it all came pouring out in an emotional flood. Everything told me that I needed to have a job and that without a job I would be out in the streets or worse. My mind literally equated having a job with survival. That's how I had programmed it for all the earlier years of my life.

FIRE YOURSELF!

It was fear that for many years kept me in jobs where I wasn't fulfilled.

In actuality the **situation turned out to be exactly the opposite of my fears.**

Without my job:
- I was actually free to think.
- I was free to pursue bigger opportunities than before.
- I wasn't limited in the amount of income I could make.
- I wasn't locked inside of an office building for eight to ten hours a day.

Best of all, I was actually OK when I left my job. It was not easy at all, but I did survive. I won't lie, because it took a lot of persistence and hard work to make it happen. There were many times I could have given up or taken a job. But, as I like to say, if you keep banging on the door of success incessantly … it eventually opens up and lets you in.

BEST OF ALL, I WAS ACTUALLY OK WHEN I LEFT MY JOB.

Going it on my own required a huge leap of faith for me. I sincerely hope it is the hardest thing I will ever have to go through in my life, because the amount of fear I had was tremendous – nearly overwhelming– until I found faith.

One of the things I have up on the wall of my office is a pencil drawing of a man looking at me. And behind the man is a drawing of another man (Jesus) with a hand on his shoulder. Above this image, the words "DO NOT BE AFRAID" are boldly printed. Here is a picture I took of that image.

In the beginning, there were many nights when I wondered if we would have to sell our home, liquidate our savings, or worse in order to keep things going; but I would look at that picture and I would try my best to stop being afraid. And I would pray and I would ask God for help and guidance. At our biggest deficit, we had just over $117,000 in credit card debt. Guess what? We survived it and ended up paying it off in full. And, regardless of where you are, you'll survive too if you keep the faith.

In the Bible it says…

Ask and ye shall receive, knock and the door
will be opened unto you.

I can now tell you that all of my prayers were answered and are still being answered today. I can't explain how some opportunities found me at just the right time, for just the right amount of money, but they did.

I strongly believe that if you come from a place of faith, you will be taken care of... not by having a bag of money drop in your lap, but through having the right circumstances, people and resources made available to you so that you can make the right decisions and take decisive action to get the results you want.

This doesn't mean that I'm never frightened at some of the things that the future will hold, but I know that if I try my hardest to always come from a place of faith, it will all work out somehow. That's an exciting way to live life and it truly allows me to enjoy every day.

Take six minutes...

...and **listen for somebody else's knock.**

Helping others requires attentiveness and focus. Often, when we help others, it's done by rote: Drop a dollar into the cup of a blind man. But listen carefully to those around you. Who is knocking? Are they being heard?

If you can hear them, answer their call. When you do, I believe that you are doing God's work here on earth.

My message of faith is a very important one that I wanted to share with you in the hope that knowledge of the power of faith can help you with whatever challenges you may be experiencing right now. And I also want you to understand how faith has worked in my life to help me achieve my goals and become an entrepreneur on an hour a day.

I would not be writing this book unless I had gotten that faith that there was something beyond me that was helping and guiding me every step along the way to push through my fear. I'm also convinced that the more responsibility I took on, and the more I opened myself to taking risk and the more faith I mustered, the more the universe opened up to help me, with the end result that things just seemed to work out.

With this in mind, I'd like to finish with a quick story that relates to an important subject near and dear to us all.

OUR HOME

The story begins when times were tough. My wife was pregnant with our second child; we were living in a two-bedroom townhouse and had no room for another child. Not to mention that this house was a tri-level home with hardwood floors and was definitely not kid friendly.

We were looking for a house close to our current location and we wanted to find a three-bedroom home. There is a development that we really like where houses are very rarely for sale. It's a gated community with very nice three- and four-bedroom homes. One day we were walking with our oldest daughter in her stroller and we saw that the gate to this community was open.

So we decided to take action and walk through the development.

Now, before this time, my wife had been praying and asking for us to find a good home. She actually sent a specific prayer for St. Philomena, the patron saint of homes.

So, here we are, walking through this development and we see a woman approaching. We say hello and start up a conversation. This leads to our mentioning that we are looking for a home in this development. *Coincidentally* (well, not really), she says that she and her husband will probably be selling their home soon.

That nice couple sold us their house for a full 10% less than market value. And they sold it to us directly, with no real estate agent. It ended up being a stressful purchase because it was contingent on our closing on our existing home, something that fell through at the last minute. That's when a friend of ours lent us $50,000 so that we could close on the new home.

Shortly afterward we sold our previous home, paid off our friend, and moved into the new place we purchased. We've been here for over seven years now, and it has been a wonderful place to raise our girls.

FAITH IS NOT LUCK

We told this story to one of our friends and I remember her saying, "Oh, that's really lucky." I actually don't think luck had anything to do with it at all. We had faith that something would happen, and the right circumstances and opportunities presented themselves to us. It wasn't easy. If we had not been able to find someone to lend us $50,000, we would have lost the house because the owners would have needed to put it on the market immediately.

So the fact is that with God's help, **we were largely responsible for our own "luck."** We were ready to go when we learned about the house and we worked diligently to make the purchase happen very quickly. We – most important – had faith, and because of our diligence, everything worked out for the best. It would not have been the same if we had not had the belief or "faith" that our dream would come true because we would have given up instead of pushing forward until we succeeded.

Whatever it is that you want, if you have faith, I firmly believe you can find it. Just realize that you need to be ready to jump when God presents that perfect opportunity for you.

> "Success is not final, failure is not fatal;
> it is the courage to continue that counts."
> – **Winston Churchill**

I hope this book inspires you to do big things with your life.

The starting gun sounded many years ago for your life. Nobody knows when it will be your turn to cross the finish line; but there is one thing we do know, we have today.

So seize the day and make the most of your life.

It is my wish that this book provides a valuable guidepost for you on your journey, and I wish you many successes.

Here's your pocket summary of what we talked about here:

- The hole you give through is the hole you receive through.
- What goes around, comes around.
- Discover faith to help fire yourself.
- Ask and ye shall receive.
- Having faith isn't the same as luck.

"Hour-a-Day Blueprint Tip"

One of the best things you can do is spend time each day in prayer. Pick up a Bible or just speak to God directly.

I like attending church, and we attend most weeks. I find it helps me get grounded and feel better about myself and my life. It also lowers my stress. Whatever works for you, spend some time thinking about what's bigger than you and listen to how you can help others, it will prove to be time very well spent.

APPENDIX A.

TEN EXTRA SECONDS OF WISDOM:

Whom you associate with is critically important –
target new people to be around daily and invest time
regularly in a supportive Mastermind Group.
Be around winners to become a winner.

THE MOST POWERFUL
GROUP IN THE WORLD

B efore I tell you about the most powerful group in the world, I'd like to clear something up. There isn't anything wrong with being in the rat race if you want and choose to be there. I know and appreciate people who work hard to provide all of the valuable services that we take for granted each and every day. We need people in these positions to keep society intact. I was a member of this group for many, many years!

HOW I CLEANED UP FOR MYSELF BY CLEANING UP FOR OTHERS

One funny story about my work experience happened when I worked in Winter Park, Colorado, during the summer of 1993.

I signed up to work at the YMCA of the Rockies for two months during my college break. It was an incredible time; I made a ton of good friends; and I worked really hard doing mostly physical labor.

Want to know what I spent the first half of my summer doing? I spent it on the housekeeping crew. Now understand, this was not a five-star resort; this was the YMCA. So I spent an entire month cleaning up after very large groups of campers. It was a tremendously humbling experience.

But of course my favorite part of the entire experience was cleaning bathrooms. If you haven't ever had the pleasure of cleaning bathrooms used by people other than your family, then you really don't know what you're missing. This gave me a real appreciation for those who work really hard to provide these basic services that we all take for granted, and I'm grateful every day that I don't have to do it myself any more!

Another job I had a few summers later was working as a waiter at a Mexican restaurant. Chi-Chi's was a big chain based on the East Coast, but it stretched all the way out to Iowa. I worked at the Chi-Chi's in West Des Moines, Iowa, which was at the time the busiest restaurant in the entire state. There I dished up endless plates of chimichangas, chips and churros – with a smile.

I really didn't know what good Mexican food was until I moved to San Diego in 1998. Now I understand that Chi-Chi's wasn't that authentic; and yes, I came to understand that guacamole is not supposed to come in a squirt bottle. **Working as a waiter allowed me to learn to appreciate serving others** and to understand how much work went into running the restaurant and being a waiter.

There is honor in *serving* other people – but it's not a shortcut to wealth. I worked very hard at being a great waiter and tried to be the best that I could be. I tracked my tips methodically and actually had the highest tip percentage of any waiter in the restaurant while working there. I firmly believed that hard work always equaled good results, so I really hustled and worked harder than almost anyone else there.

IT'S NOT JUST HARD WORK THAT LEADS TO SUCCESS; IT'S WORKING SMARTER AND WORKING ON THE RIGHT THINGS.

I tell these stories so you will understand that I did not have an entrepreneurial upbringing. I was very much conditioned to get a job and to appreciate the value of hard work, regardless of what I was doing.

Since then, I've grown to understand **that it's not just hard work that leads to success; it's working smarter and working on the right things.** I can be the best waiter in the world that has the highest tip percentage of anyone, anywhere; but I'm still not going to be a millionaire next year because of that. This employment path was *definitely not for me.*

I absolutely can't stand the idea of working for other people and making *them* rich, all the while knowing that they can fire me anytime they want. I understood even then that being a waiter – or even working for other people – would not lead me down the road to the entrepreneurial and financial freedom I was looking for.

THE ROAD OF AN ENTREPRENEUR IS *NOT* FOR EVERYONE

You need to make that decision for yourself, and nobody else can or should make it for you. As for me, I was determined not to take the route of the rat race; and early on I began looking for a proven road to get out of it, but I was too scared to take any action toward my goal until I was in my mid-30s.

Dad's last transfer was to Des Moines, Iowa, where he worked for two years before becoming unemployed. Now he found himself in the Midwest with two children nearing college age and not a lot of savings. While I never talked to him in detail about the decision process he went through, I knew that he was sick and tired of working for somebody else. That's when he decided to purchase a company of his own.

He bought a small architectural millwork company in West Des Moines. It was a wood and cabinet manufacturing company that makes cabinets, cash register stations, countertops, and other custom millwork that goes primarily into businesses and office buildings. My father ended up with a lifestyle business that he kept nearly 20 years.

As an aside, he and my mother have been happily married for more than 40 years and recently retired onto a 43-foot trawler called Queen Ann's Revenge. They are currently cruising America's Great Loop throughout the eastern United States.

I remember having a conversation with my father when I was still in high school. He had always worked for someone else his entire life and had been bounced from city to city and across the country throughout his career. It always seemed to me like a reactionary way of living. You have no control yourself when you allow a company to dictate your future.

The important point I'm making here is that my father decided to get his own company only *after* he lost his last job. I still remember talking to him about a year after he had bought the new company. His comment to me was interesting. "Son," he said, "if I have one regret in life, it's that I didn't decide to go out on my own a long time ago. This sure beats working for someone else." He had a picture on the wall of a successful businessman on the front of a magazine cover – I believe it was *Inc.* magazine. The gist of the caption was this, "Bob left the corporate world to go out on his own. And boy is he glad."

Take 45 minutes…

…and **make a practical list of three businesses** you could enter tomorrow and have a chance of succeeding. Make a note of your strengths after each one. Be realistic, but don't allow negative thinking to intrude.

Now, make another set of notes explaining to yourself why you haven't done any of the things on the list. No excuses – just explanations.

Finally, **choose one option and overcome those explanations.** You're on your way!

Amazing, but as I look back on my time with my dad, I remember several key conversations with him and letters that he sent me throughout the years; but that conversation in particular was a big one, because it really summed up what he was all about at that time in his life. **He was sick and tired of making other people**

rich and decided to try to make himself rich. It was very inspiring to see someone I knew very well go through that kind of personal transformation.

IF I HAD KNOWN EVERYTHING I'M NOW PUTTING IN THIS BOOK, I COULD HAVE DONE IT EVEN SOONER

As I developed the theories for my hour-a-day strategy, I began to diligently study success, money-making, entrepreneurship and marketing in order to expand my own skill set.

And... it worked! My plan, which I literally figured out as I went along, got me out of the corporate rat race in just a couple of years. **If I had known everything I'm now putting in this book, I could have done it even sooner!**

As an entrepreneur, I own and am involved in several different, profitable businesses in multiple niches. I am also a highly paid marketing strategist, able to show those frustrated with the rat race or those who have businesses that are imprisoning them how to stop the endless treadmill of the rat race – once and for all. This allows my clients to take back their lives, finances and *freedom*.

One way I do that is by **sharing the incredibly valuable secrets I discovered that you, too, can put to use for yourself.** The reason I can help you is because I was right where you are – working too hard, making someone else wealthy, and ready to take my life to the next level. And, if you already have a successful business, I can relate to that as well.

There's an amazing story, told by a friend of mine, that revolves around making this change. Craig was the first friend I met when I moved to San Diego. I had known him for a few years when he told me that he had just left a job and was looking for a new position. He was trying to get an interview in a certain commercial real estate company, but they were giving him the runaround.

He really couldn't believe it, but they weren't hiring him right away.

There's something you need to understand if you aren't familiar with these types of commercial real estate sales positions: They are 100% commission. So this company really had no reason *not* to hire him. In fact, Craig could have walked into a number of firms and settled right in, but this particular firm was the one that he was really keen on joining.

MY FRIEND AND THE STORY OF LIVING A "GOOD LIFE"

Craig leased the absolute best-to-be-found, low-rent house, half a block from Crystal Pier in Pacific Beach, San Diego. We nicknamed him "Good Life" because he truly lived the good live, spending a lot of time surfing and traveling – living right on the beach in sunny PB. It was a place his friends liked to visit and it was about one of those friends—a friend who was already self-employed—that Craig related this story.

During the time Craig was looking for his new job, a friend came over to visit. As the friend was leaving, he said something that stuck in Craig's mind and then later stuck in my mind when Craig relayed the story to me. As he walked out, Craig's friend said to him,

"You know, I made up my mind when I was going out on my own that I'm not going to be anyone's bitch anymore." And on that note he walked out and slammed the door behind him.

Please pardon his language, but I hope the impact of this statement rings true to you. Here it is in very plain English:

YOU CAN'T EXPECT TO GET RICH IF YOU SPEND YOUR TIME MAKING OTHER PEOPLE RICH.

Basically, Craig's friend was saying that he was done working for someone else and being a slave to the system. He was, in essence, stepping off the grid and taking control and responsibility for his own life from that point forward.

My friend Craig ended up – on that very day – opening up a phone book to cold-call apartment building owners. One call landed him his first big apartment real estate deal in La Jolla. Not only that, but Craig parlayed that purchase into a sale at the top of the market into a real estate exchange, delivering him with funds that he used to invest in a great apartment building in Las Vegas. That apartment property happened to be next door to the Las Vegas Convention Center. And guess who came knocking to expand their parking facilities a few short months after Craig purchased the apartment building?

Craig sold that property less than one year after purchasing it. Here's a quote from the article in the *Las Vegas Sun*:

For the second time in three months, the Las Vegas Convention and Visitors Authority has snapped up an apartment complex on nearby Sierra Vista Drive for more than $10 million – assuring a windfall profit for the owner who flipped the parcel, depleting the number of affordable rental units in the area.

Still, LVCVA officials praised Tuesday's unanimous board decision to purchase the 76-unit Sierra Madre apartment complex at 454 Sierra Vista Drive for $10.87 million as a thrifty purchase given skyrocketing real estate values in recent months.

The LVCVA purchased Sierra Madre from Rubin & Associates, a San Diego firm that invests in real estate. Rubin, who owned Sierra Madre through a limited liability corporation registered with the Nevada secretary of state, purchased the complex on April 5 for $6.25 million. That means he turned a $4.62 million profit on an eight-month investment.

Today, let's just say that he is very comfortable, thanks to the other investments he made from his profits on this deal.

This was an absolute home-run deal for my friend, because he took decisive action to become an entrepreneur.

Take 7 minutes...

...and **think about what you're worth.**

Look at Craig's example. How many years of working for someone else do you think it would take you to make $4.62 million?

What if you make $50,000 a year?

Answer: To reach $4.62 million it would take you 92.4 years. And that's only if you work every single day of your life, including all of your childhood and retirement years.

What if you are a six-figure earner making $10,000 a month, or $120,000 a year?

Answer: It would take you 38.5 years. Coincidentally, that's how old I am as I write this book; and so that means I would had to have worked every year of my entire life making six figures annually to equal that sum. To an average working person who began working at age 20 and worked to age 65, that would amount to almost his or her entire career, especially if you took out vacation days and time off.

When you let that really sink in, it shows you **money is really nothing more than an idea,** in this case a real estate idea quickly and decisively acted on by my friend Craig – an idea that ended up being a life-changer for him and his family.

ONE DECISION OR ONE THOUGHT CAN MAKE ALL THE DIFFERENCE

All of Craig's success came from making a decision one fateful day when his friend walked down the stairs saying something in an offhand manner that turned out to be significant for Craig, and then slammed the door. The friend left, but he left his thought behind with Craig.

These kinds of stories propelled me to actively begin my search for another way… a better way. And by living the program I discovered, I found that not only was I able to exit the rat race, I've been able to achieve the freedom I was looking for and have been able to escape from being a slave to the system.

Don't get me wrong, going out on my own was a leap of faith and was very difficult for me personally, even with this great secret that I'll be sharing with you. It was especially hard because I had a wife who was staying at home with our two young children, and we were living in San Diego, an expensive city, and had our kids in a private school. But this same decision enabled me to spend more time with my family, earn more money faster and more easily, gain more energy, meet incredible people, grow tremendously, and love living every single day and minute of my life.

I really didn't get the "leap" part until I actually had made the leap, but it's all part of the process.

The environment I grew up in was very non-entrepreneurial until I was finishing high school and my dad made the change into being his own boss. The message he told me didn't register strongly enough at the young age of 16, so I went onward into my own corporate rat race for nearly 15 long years after college.

Boy, I sure wish that I had figured out these things a lot sooner.

Because now, **since I've made this leap, everything has changed!**

But I remember how it felt in the beginning. When I made the jump, I was more than terrified: I was nearly petrified. Of course, you may have already made the jump and are looking for an edge to go even further. As for me, I was frozen solid as a block of ice and unable to take action.

Take a quarter-hour…

And **learn how to read some simple signs.**

Not everything in life is spelled out so clearly, but signs that you're on the wrong road are easy to spot:

Your blood pressure is high.

You wake at 5 a.m. stressed and afraid.

Your family is less in your life than your work.

You don't have time to question the "why?" of what you're doing.

You're late everywhere you go – for no good reason.

If you see any of these signs along the way, you can safely assume that all of them mean one thing: "time out, slow down."

However, God did send me a few signs along the way. The fact that you now find yourself reading this book may be one of those signs for you.

Here is an incident that was a sign for me.

On a flight I remember in particular – during my college years – I received a strong hint that it was not unheard of to take risks and set out to do your own thing. On the plane I met a gentleman who had just started up his own company in computer cabling, a very low-tech, low-margin business – but he was doing it.

Not only that, he had three kids as well. Not one, not two, but *three* kids! Surprisingly to me, he didn't express a single fear. I remember being almost incredulous at this. How could he have the audacity? How could he have the courage not to be scared to death?

How in the heck is he *doing* this?

He was coming from a place of confidence and faith. It was hard to believe that he was doing this – it seemed so very, very *risky* to me. It actually seemed foolish and stupid as well.

In reality, it was anything but risky, foolish or stupid. **He believed in himself, believed in his plan, and was going to do what it took to make it happen.** I was too paralyzed to take action and thus amazed by his story at the time, but for me it was another small seed that was planted.

It would take until years later before that seed actually began to sprout, but I'd like to thank this gentleman who pointed me in the right direction so many years ago on that long flight.

It was hearing stories about risk takers and seeing this kind of blind faith that really helped me get over my fears as I went through my own transitions and movement from being a corporate guy, scared out of my mind of being on my own, to becoming, as I am today, an entrepreneur.

Was there any one thing that made a really big impact as I went on this journey?

The answer is… yes!

And that's what I'll be introducing to you right now.

THE ENTREPRENEUR'S TURNING POINT: MY DISCOVERY OF THE *MOST POWERFUL GROUP IN THE WORLD*

So the seed was planted; I began to grow more discontented at working for somebody else. This meant that I was constantly looking to add new skills and opportunities that would help me become an entrepreneur, constantly trying to find the best option for me to make my transition and be better able to provide for my family.

Having some real estate experience and a real estate background, I first looked at doing real estate deals, and we actually closed a few deals. However, the turning point came from somewhere else.

In my previous career, I had worked for the world's largest commercial real estate company, but had decided to leave at the turn of the millennium because I really had a passion for technology and I wanted to get involved in a technology company. I went to work for an internet web services provider as a project manager. This was during the dot-com heyday and we were super busy helping startup companies get their online presence. As I came up to speed, I moved over into sales and finally was the sales manager before leaving for greener pastures.

I wasn't there very long, but I was able to quickly learn the ropes of working in high-tech. The good news was that **I really enjoyed the** change and I liked being someone who understood sales, marketing and technology. That gave me a big leg up on everyone else.

My next stop was a hardware company that manufactured GPS equipment. I was the international marketing manager and also managed the customer service team. My entire team and I got "right-sized" about a year later.

I REALLY ENJOYED THE CHANGE AND I LIKED BEING SOMEONE WHO UNDERSTOOD SALES, MARKETING AND TECHNOLOGY.

I remember the feeling of helplessness that almost overwhelmed me as I met with the controller who let me go that day. I was mad because during my employment with the company I had saved one of its biggest accounts, and I knew I had done an excellent job in the U.S. and in Europe. I felt powerless. The decision had come from the parent company in Korea. It had nothing to do with me or anybody else on my team; the company was just restructuring.

That experience helped me decide that I wasn't going to work for just any company at my next position; I would be selective in what I chose. A few short months later, I settled in at a locally owned software company where I was the director of business development. Here, I single-handedly closed all of the company's biggest accounts with organizations such as Southwest Airlines, Wells Fargo, ADP, the FBI, the Office of Homeland Security, and the Executive Office of the President of the United States.

Take 10 minutes...

...and **calculate your vulnerabilities.**

To succeed as an entrepreneur, you have to control events the same way you control finances. Here's a simple calculator if you already have a business:

1. Is your customer base/client list growing?
   Yes___ No ___ Don't know ___

2. Can you confidently predict what your business will look like in 12 months?
   Yes___ No___ Don't know ___

3. Is your business success predicated on your personal well-being?
   Yes___ No___ Don't know ___

4. Is your business' stability reliant on one key person or one client?
   Yes___ No___ Don't know ___

5. Are your finances sufficient? Or are you living on the edge? _____

Each question is worth 20 points.
Answers: 1: Yes. 2: Yes. 3: No. 4: No. 5: Sufficient.
If your score is less than 60, your vulnerabilities are serious, and you could easily find yourself reacting to events rather than directing them.

I was doing a lot of traveling back to the East Coast at that time as well. I later became that company's vice president of sales and led a team of more than a dozen sales and support staff. We grew that company more than 2,000% over nearly eight years, funded almost exclusively by selling and without venture capital investment.

It was about half way through my time in working with that software company that it began to sink in that I would probably get some great results if I learned more about the internet and selling online, especially since we were selling millions of dollars worth of software annually. I was certain my experience would be a real asset to online sales – especially if I could find the help and insights I needed to stay in control of whatever happened next.

THE SECRETS OF MASTERMIND

At this pivotal point in my life, as I began to look for ways to find financial and personal freedom away from the rat race, I was about to discover a secret that I'm going to share with you in just a moment.

A secret that...

- Can help you accelerate your business and maintain control of events.
- Can free you from the rat race.
- That nearly ALL successful people point to as a key reason for their success.

I learned this secret during a hot and humid October weekend in Tampa, Florida, several years ago when I traveled across the county to my first internet seminar.

And during that seminar, I decided to join my very first Mastermind group.

The concept of the Mastermind group was formally introduced by Napoleon Hill in the early 1900s. In his book, the timeless classic, *Think and Grow Rich*, he wrote about the Mastermind principle as this:

"The coordination of knowledge and effort of two or more people, who work toward a definite purpose, in the spirit of harmony…"

He also said, "No two minds ever come together without thereby creating a third, invisible intangible force, which may be likened to a third mind."

In a Mastermind group, the agenda belongs to the group, and each person's participation is key. Your peers give you feedback, help you brainstorm new possibilities, and set up accountability structures that keep you focused and on track.

This creates a community of supportive members who brainstorm together to move the group to new heights. Each member gains tremendous insights, which can improve both their business and personal life. I liken a Mastermind group to having an objective board of directors that is available to help you with any business challenge that you may experience. The information and support you can gain through a group like this is key to maintaining control of the events you will face as an entrepreneur.

MASTERMIND GROUPS ARE A HUGE "SECRET" OF THE MOST SUCCESSFUL

You can realize many wonderful benefits inside of a properly designed Mastermind group. For instance, you will be able to...

- Leverage the group's connection and experience.
- Grow your own experience, skill and confidence.
- Get measurable progress in your business and in your personal life.
- Benefit from a shared camaraderie and knowing that you are not alone.

All of these equal "control" of your life and work.

TWO Q'S AND TWO A'S

1. Who would be ideal candidates for a Mastermind group?

- Those who have a similar interests.
- Those who have growing their businesses as a goal.
- Those who see the benefit of having a supportive team of Mastermind members.
- Those who want to reach their goals faster and more easily.

2. How do Mastermind groups work?

Mastermind groups can meet in person, on the telephone, or via online collaboration software. Most groups typically meet once a month. The core Mastermind session is usually structured in 20- or 30-minute individual increments. That means that each person will have the entire group focused on his or her business during that time.

The interesting thing about Mastermind groups is that you usually end up learning much more from hearing others discuss their business than when you are discussing your own.

JOINING A MASTERMIND GROUP WAS THE SINGLE BIGGEST THING I DID TO ACCELERATE MY BUSINESS AND ALLOW ME TO EXIT THE RAT RACE.

There's nothing that a small group of committed people cannot help you get through more quickly and easily than you could if you had to figure it out on your own.

HE WHO HESITATES IS NOT GOING TO WIN THE RACE

It was a huge stepping stone for me and made a tremendous difference in my personal development and my business success. It was literally a *different path* I choose that day that led me toward a very different life from the one I had led until then – a better path... a path of freedom, unlimited financial opportunity, meeting exciting new people, and living a fantastic, faith-filled life with family and friends. Of course, it also meant hard decisions, stressful times and change that was not easy for me at all. But, it also did something very, very important as well. It introduced me to the power of the Mastermind.

We all find that we actually have much more greatness inside of ourselves than we give ourselves credit for.

I was one of those people who had *not* read *Think and Grow Rich* by Napoleon Hill. I had a copy but I hadn't read it. I think on some level I was scared of what I would find inside myself once I read the book.

I had never even heard of a Mastermind meeting before, but when I heard these magic words...

"You are the sum of the five friends closest to you..."

...it was the wake-up call that I needed to get some new friends who were more successful than I was. And I did get those friends by joining my very first Mastermind Group... *before I could afford it.*

Most important to me is how I grew as a person – growth that I know will be worth millions more to me over the next few years.

When I join Mastermind groups today, I like to find groups that meet monthly, and ideally are in the Southwest US. This means regular accountability as well as not having to get on a plane and travel cross-country for the meetings.

WHAT DOES THIS SECRET HAVE TO DO WITH YOU?

Well, I can tell you that the single biggest thing responsible for my getting out of the rat race, for giving me the opportunity to spend more time with my two young girls, for being able to enjoy life more, is the power of the Mastermind group.

It is my considered opinion that:
- Going to seminars doesn't get near the results of a properly run Mastermind.
- Reading books or listening to CDs won't come close to giving the same benefits that a Mastermind will.
- Personal coaching, while valuable and necessary, can't hold a candle to the Mastermind.

If you are serious about:
- *Really* accelerating your business and creating the freedom and lifestyle you want (and you need to think about this because some people aren't ready for big success).
- Making more progress in the next 12 months than in the previous 12 years.
- Upgrading the "five closest people to you" to real movers and shakers who are making things happen every month.

If you're ready to stop talking about change and progress and ready to start making it happen then the answer is simple. Let me repeat it again:

You absolutely must join a Mastermind group.

I know what you may be thinking – what if I don't have the funds or the time to invest in something like this? Well, it takes some energy to get the fuel ignited. You can start off convincing those more successful than you to get together once a week or once a month.

And if you're thinking you can't find the time, think again. We all can find the time to get involved in a group like this when we follow the strategies that I outline in the Time Management portion of this book. Just a few strategy enhancements in how you manage your time can make a huge difference and free up plenty of time to do what you want to do.

WHAT KIND OF GROUP SHOULD I JOIN?

You need to join one somewhere run by somebody who knows and understands how they work, how to facilitate them, and also is *already successful.*

I couldn't recommend the GKIC Mastermind groups more. And if you're lucky enough to live in an area that has a local Glazer-Kennedy Independent Business Advisor, then you need to get in touch with him or her and get involved today.

Here are three very important reasons these GKIC groups in particular are worth investigating:

They are professionally run, local groups – and, as I found out, odds are you will not find many high-level Mastermind groups meeting in your city. "Local group" means you will get local attention from other local business owners, and you can save travel money while staying in your hometown.

Access to high-powered marketing experts. Not only do you get local expertise from someone who walks the walk and talks the talk, you also get access to Dan Kennedy. Dan is one of the most celebrated marketing strategists in the world and the world's highest-paid copywriter. He "visits" these Mastermind groups via DVD each month, and the lessons he gives are incredibly valuable – and you won't find them anywhere else. I think he has personally trained more first-time millionaires than anyone else alive.

The best investment you can make in these tough times is in yourself. You are the only one capable of giving yourself a bailout during these hard financial times, and you can do it by making bold steps forward – sometimes scary steps, but ones that will pave a path of prosperity for you into the future. But you must choose to act and take advantage of opportunity when you see it.

When you are ready to take your business, your career and your life to the next level, the power of the Mastermind simply cannot be beat or matched any other way for helping you achieve that goal.

So, I swallowed hard and decided to go for it. All I can say is, "Thank goodness I did; it has proven to be the best move I've ever made for myself, for my family, for my business and for my life." I would like to give you my highest recommendation to find a Mastermind group as soon as you possibly can. I wholeheartedly believe that joining one of these groups, even a less-costly one that requires a more nominal monthly investment, can have a similar effect on you.

A professionally run, local Mastermind group is actually much better, particularly when you are beginning your business, because the facilitator has experience in these kinds of situations, even though you don't, and your success will be greatly accelerated with a monthly, local meeting.

I run multiple high-end Mastermind groups and have been tapped by some of the world's best-known thought leaders to partner with them to help develop their own Mastermind programs. To discover more, you can watch an informative video online that explains more about these powerful groups.

www.HourADayBook.com/Mastermind

Here's your pocket summary of what we talked about here:

- Choose who you associate with.
- Be around winners to become a winner.
- There is honor in serving others.
- The path of an entrepreneur isn't for everyone.
- One decision or one thought can make all the difference.
- Join a mastermind - the most powerful group in the world.

Your "Hour-a-Day Blueprint Tip"

So how do you get started in finding a Mastermind group in only an hour a day? Well, you can start with joining a professional group like I did (see above) or you can just start your own.

The important thing is to make sure you are around peers – or those actually doing as good or better than you – and then you need to make sure you meet on a regular basis.

Mastermind groups that only meet sporadically or randomly are not the ones that you want to be a part of. You want to be meeting regularly and you want to make sure everyone is there to help the rest of the members. One selfish or non-giving member can ruin the entire group.

And, if you start it up, guess what? You can add or subtract people as you wish.

APPENDIX B.

"So the last day you're in the office before you go
on a trip, how much work do you get done and how
productive are you? For most people it's
two to five times more productive
than they are normally and the reason is they have a
deadline and they know that they have to focus
and get things done…
Can you set a deadline for yourself this week
to get a nagging project off your plate?"

QUESTIONS AND ANSWERS WITH THE HOUR-A-DAY ENTREPRENEUR

As I was finishing this book, I thumbed back through and wondered what else I could do to make my message clearer.

Then I remembered a remarkable conversation I'd had with a true entrepreneurial pioneer, Jim Palmer. He calls himself the "newsletter guru" because – well, that's his specialty, producing high-quality, customer-retaining newsletters for himself and his clients. Among innovative entrepreneurs, he's very well-known and very widely read – and among the wittiest and most insightful men I know. When we met, creative sparks flew. I'm sure you'll pick up some great words of wisdom from our meeting, so here is what it sounded like:

JIM PALMER:

*Well, hello there everyone.   This is **Jim Palmer, the Newsletter Guru.** I'd like to welcome you to another great "Interview the Experts Coaching Call."*

My very special guest expert this month is none other than Henry Evans. Henry is the president and CEO of Timezone Marketing, amongst a host of other businesses and operations and he's a marketing and business building expert, which is one of the reasons I think we get along so well. So this is going to be a good call. It's going to be a fun call. There's going to be something on here for everybody.

*We are ready to go with this month's topic, which is **how to become a successful entrepreneur in just one hour a day.** And let me tell you a little bit about my very special guest, Henry Evans. He is an entrepreneur, a self-described geek and marketer, sales guru, teacher, husband, father to two really, really great girls. Henry has been active in sales and marketing, in the sales and marketing arena probably for about 20 years now. And like I do with all of my guests, or the ones that I can Google, I've done a little bit of my own research and come up with something other than what I see in his bio.*

Henry grew up in Youngstown, New York, which had a population of 1,872 including Henry, and he first learned how to program a Radio Shack color computer at the age of 8. And I think that's where the self-described geek comes in. He was also the first student in his entire school district to do a report printed on a home PC, and that was in the fifth grade.

He began his sales and marketing career on the street selling The Buffalo Evening Times at the age of 14. You know, as I said, Henry's not just a preacher of strategy and business philosophy. He's been active on the frontlines and in leadership capacities in software companies, hardware companies, commercial real estate firms, manufacturing organizations. He's sold everything from newspapers to office buildings and kitchen remodeling and even software licenses. He's been able to excel in all these different fields because, from what I've observed, he's just got a great combination of sales and marketing savvy. And he's got a little bit of that geeky technical aptitude, and the thing I like about Henry the most, he's got a make-it-happen attitude. And that's why I admire him so much.

Henry has had responsibility for generating over $15 million in sales. He's engineered a $189,000 payday in 90 minutes. He's done everything, from working in Washington, D.C., to all over the place. Just to let you know, I first met Henry a few years ago, and he's one of the nicest guys on the planet. We became instant friends and actually in full disclosure I'll tell you Henry is a member in my monthly Mastermind and coaching program. And without further ado and at the risk of giving him a slightly swelled head, I'm going to stop right there and say, Henry, welcome to the call.

HENRY EVANS:

Hey, thanks, Jim. I'm glad to be here. I'll tell you, after that intro I don't think I need to say anything. I don't think I've ever sounded so good. So that was great. Thank you.

JIM PALMER:

We'll just close out here folks.

HENRY EVANS:

Exactly.

JIM PALMER:

Henry, let me tell people why the title of today's call is "How to become a successful entrepreneur in one hour a day," because that is pretty close to what the title of your new book is, which I'm just thrilled. I mean everybody that listens to me knows I'm constantly saying, get a book done, get a book done. And you are getting a book done. So if that's not the title, I know it's coming out like very, very soon. Have you settled on the final title yet?

HENRY EVANS:

*It is. The final title is **The Hour-a-Day Entrepreneur**. So how to get out of the rat race and achieve entrepreneurial freedom with only one focused hour a day, which really is based on the true story of me doing exactly that while I was still working at a corporate job. I actually was spending an hour a day after coming home from a full-time vice president-level position, and would spend time with my family and then from 9 to 10 at night, every single day and usually a few hours on Saturday, I basically was able to ramp up a side business that allowed me to leave the corporate world and leave the rat race. And I haven't looked back and have four successful businesses now and just love being an entrepreneur. It was a hard move, but it was worth it, and I have so many people asking me how I did it. So the book's really an answer to that. If you're somebody that is an entrepreneur or wants to be an entrepreneur, it's really meant to short-cut that process for you.*

JIM PALMER:

It's a great book. I'll let people know that I did read a draft copy. It's wonderful. It's a fun read because it's written in kind of a storyteller format. But there are some serious good business lessons in there. One of the expressions I like, Henry, because I coach a lot of people and one of the common themes is how do you get more done and how do I do this. And I think what actually stops most people is starting.

So that's why I kind of loved the theme of your book. Now you went to work, you came home, I'm sure you had family time and helped with putting the kids to bed and whatever else. And then, like you said, from 9 to 10 or probably 10 to 11 you got started on your business while you were still an employee. So that's kind of the theme. So I really like that. I mean that's one of the big lessons for a lot of people. You know what? Just start. So, let me ask you this. Why did you decide to write the book in the first place?

HENRY EVANS:

Well, it really came, Jim, from having people ask me, hey, how did you do that? Because a lot of people end up spinning their wheels when they work 40 hours a week or 50 hours a week or if you're an entrepreneur, 90 or 100 hours a week sometimes, and end up not getting a lot done. So they're not very effective or efficient with their time. And so the book was engineered to show how I've become very effective. And I did it mainly because I had to. And I always use the example... think about the last time you went on vacation and right before you left or went away on a business trip, but it's ideally before a big vacation, think about the day before you leave.

*So the last day you're in the office before you go on a trip, how much work do you get done and how productive are you? And for most people it's two to five times more productive than they are normally and the reason is they have a deadline and **they know that they have to focus and get things done.***

So I was able to get done and ramp up a business really doing one hour a day and I think getting as much done as most people who work a full eight hours a day, literally, in one-eighth of the time because I didn't *have a choice. And it's all the specific strategies that I've used. I'm happy to share some of those as well if you want to go into that. But **I literally outlined all the best strategies I used.** And not a lot of them are original thought. I'm a big proponent of modeling.*

So I look at people that are successful and I look at what they've done and I model them. I look at how you've been able to author several books. And so when I wanted to get my book done, call up people like you and people like Bill Glazer. You guys already have books done. So model what you've already done. But what was the real impetus for doing it was to put down in writing how I did it because I get asked so often, how did you do that on one hour a day when I can't do it on eight hours a day. And so it's a short cut guide, if you will.

JIM PALMER:

It's awesome and you know success leaves tracks. So I love that modeling philosophy. There's no need to reinvent anything pretty much.

And one of the things you said, Henry, is about deadlines. They're critical. I mean, what is it? "Goals without deadlines are dreams." Deadlines are huge as a way to get things done.

HENRY EVANS:

*They're just critical and people don't get things done. I was just at a very large event over the weekend. I was speaking to about 750 people and I had several people come up after – and I was talking about time management. And several people came up and they were asking me the questions that you just did. Hey, I set deadlines and I don't fulfill on the deadlines. And you just said two very important things, which is having an accountability partner is one thing that works really, really well. The other thing that I love to do that really works is **people are always motivated by one of two things. It's either increasing pleasure*** *or decreasing pain.* *And I recommend if you really want to get results, you have to do both.*

So the way to do that and getting something done is say that you have to get a newsletter out or you have to get a marketing piece out, whatever it might be, you set the deadline. And if you don't get it done, there's some penalty that happens. And if you do, there's some reward that happens.

So, one of the ones that I've taken on for myself is if I don't get something done, fortunately I haven't had this happen yet, but I really like my sleep. My two girls were born 13 months apart and so I didn't sleep for two and a half years straight. And so I like to get a full night sleep. And so if I don't get something done, I set my alarm for 2 in the morning and I have to get up and take a walk. And that for me is all the incentive I need. That's more pain than a Chinese water torture. So, that works. And then you put something good on there as well. So for me it might be taking my wife for a trip to Las Vegas, or a trip to Palm Desert, or taking the kids out for a sail or a boat ride, whatever it might be. You put something really good and fun in there as well. But for most people they are not their own best clients. Their clients and their customers and prospects and family, everybody else comes first, and they leave themselves with whatever time is left.

And yet to flip flop that, if you want to truly get more done, you have to be on the offensive and you have to go first. So your time comes first and you work on that stuff when you first start your day, and you don't let other people dictate your schedule.

JIM PALMER:

That's great. Henry, let's talk about the hour-a-day kind of name and the theme for the book, why the hour-a-day part? Why is that important?

HENRY EVANS:

Right, well, that for me ended up being what I did. So, I mean, I ended up starting a company from basically zero, an online business, and we ramped it up to just over $30,000 a month and it was literally on an hour a day. And so that's kind of where the book name came from. Mainly because people would talk about what I was getting done and I was joining Mastermind groups when I first started doing this. This is about four years ago now. And several people in the Mastermind group were like, "Boy, you're sure getting a lot done. How are you doing that when you're still working full time?" And I said, "Well I'm doing it in an hour a day because that's all I have." And they started nicknaming me the hour-a-day guy. And so that name kind of stuck and so then I figured I'd carry that through when I wrote the book. And so the book really is the hour-a-day entrepreneur, and it's how I did it.

Now that I'm full-time in the entrepreneurial realm, I definitely work quite a bit more than that. Now, I could scale back if I wanted to but I have four businesses now instead of one, which I guess means I can spend two hours a day on each. **But I just wanted people to know that it's not about the quantity of time. It's the quality.** *And so the hour a day is really why I chose that and also why I chose the name of my company, which is Timezone Marketing.*

*I'm just fanatical about time, using time properly, instead of it using you. Bill Gates, Warren Buffet. And kind of a funny story Warren Buffet actually owns the Buffalo Evening News, which is now The Buffalo News, which was my first job. So actually my first job I worked for the world's greatest investor, which I just found out recently, which I thought was pretty cool. But it all stems from getting more done in a short amount of time. And the idea of getting more done in an hour than most people get done all day seems to be a pretty compelling offer that people like and want to achieve. You look at what Tim Ferriss has done with **The***

4-Hour Work Week. It's kind of similar to that. So I kind of hope that that kind of got to the answer to the question there.

JIM PALMER:

It does. And one of the reasons I like it is because if people think about, well if I'm going to launch this business it's going to take me nine months, or it's going to take 2,000 hours, whatever it is. It becomes so unmanageable in their mind and, you know, another expression I guess is how to eat an elephant one bite at a time.

HENRY EVANS:

Exactly.

JIM PALMER:

I love the fact that you're going to encourage people to just get started one hour at a time because people can do that. *I think the theme is really going to resonate with a lot of people.*

HENRY EVANS:

Absolutely. And I was just saying that I'd be willing to bet you that on those days that you get up early and you work two focused hours in a time block, which is one thing I teach. **I'm adamant about focused time blocks. No email, no BlackBerry, no distraction, no beeping Outlook alarms or anything else. I bet you end up getting more done in those two hours than you do the rest of the day.**

JIM PALMER:

It is incredible. It is so awesome how much I get done. Now, I end up falling asleep at 8:30, 9, and I keep the cycle going. Those productive hours are incredible because there's nothing else going on. It's also – and it's different for different people. But for me that's also my most creative time, when I first wake up, because, typically, once your brain really fully wakes up and gets in gear, it starts going into task mode instead of creative mode. So I like to take advantage of that time.

So let me ask you this. My kids are all grown and gone now, but there wasn't a long time before, just like you, when I had four young ones at home, and there was soccer, and band, and dance, and choir and music and God knows what else we had in our lives. But suppose someone only has 15 minutes a day, can they still make this work for them?

HENRY EVANS:

I would think that you can. Now, I actually recommend spending 15 minutes in the morning doing a daily routine where — I mean just to be very tactical with you, what I do and I've modeled this from people that are very, very successful and taken what I really like from it — but I always write down in the morning what I'm most grateful for, so my family, my faith, my health, my businesses. I get to live in San Diego and I grew up in Buffalo. So that's a nice place to hang your hat. So I go through all the things I'm grateful for. And then I list off, and I always look at my goals for the month, my goals for the week. And then what are the three things, if I get nothing else done today, what are the three things I'm going to do. And I start on the first thing until I get it done, and then the second thing until I get it done, and then the third thing until I get it done.

*And I try my best not to get distracted at all. And so that means never ever starting the day with email, because that's the worst place you can begin your day. And when I do that, **when I spend that 15 minutes and set my day up that way it's just absolutely incredible.***

So that's kind of my minimum of personal planning time for the day, which is what I recommend for people that ask that, hey, look I've only got 15 minutes to kind of get my act together during the day. That's what I recommend is you start off with the gratitude, and you start off with your list of what your goals are. And then always keep in mind why you're doing what you're doing. Are you working on things that have high impact or high-income potential as opposed to busywork? And I find that that's just critical.

Every day I do that, I have a productive day whether I work one hour, two hours, four hours or 12 hours, I have a good day. And the days I don't do that are the days, I kind of call it, I'm going into the defensive mode. You know, when you're playing football and the team has the lead, and so they put two people on the line and everybody else is protecting against the pass, it's called the prevent defense. Well, you aren't going to score anything when you're in the prevent defense. And usually the other team is going to march right down the field. You're just protecting against getting scored on instead of going on the offense. And so if I don't spend those 15 minutes a day planning it out, I end up being on the defensive the rest of the day and I don't get nearly as much done.

So if somebody just has 15 minutes, that's exactly what I'd recommend that, they try doing. And probably be pretty surprised how you think, "Well, I'm spending 15 minutes here. That's kind of a waste of time." But in reality it's going to save you way more time than you invest.

JIM PALMER:

That's wonderful. And I really like what you said about the attitude of gratitude. That is huge because really, if it's the first thing you think of when you wake up and the last thing you think of when you go to sleep, it really, really has a big impact on your mind. Like anything, that's one of those 21-day things. So if you can do it for 21 days, you'll really be surprised how your mind-set changes.

HENRY EVANS:

Especially if you focus on it.

JIM PALMER:

Yeah, the day and age we're living in now there's plenty to worry about, but if you just focus on your things you're grateful for, it really helps your mind-set. What do you think the top three skills are that someone needs to become a more successful entrepreneur?

HENRY EVANS:

*Well, **the number one skill is focus.** There's no question because I've hung out — so I was somebody that I interviewed all of my family's most successful friends, all of my friends' parents who were most successful when I got out of college. And I actually got quite a few job offers mainly because I was doing informational interviews. But I've really made it a study of what makes people more successful and helps them get more done. And I would say the number-one thing is focus.*

You have to be able to focus on one thing at a time and not be distracted and not go down rabbit trails, as I've heard them called. So, for example, if somebody starts doing one thing and they say, "Oh, well, I need to check and see if I can get that flight." So they go onto the website to check the flight and they see that somebody has pinged them with a Facebook update. And then before you know it an hour has gone by. So it's the focus, being able to do one thing at a time.

*The second thing, — which I've only recently figured out and I've got to give you credit on this, Jim, because you really helped me figure this out, too — which is **you have to get rid of the tasks that don't work well for you,** and you specifically told me about email. And so I actually have an assistant now who's based in San Diego, best thing I've ever done, and she's handling all of my email. And you'd be amazed how your stress goes* down when you lower that. Now, I used to have a virtual assistant who would do that for me and that's definitely better than doing it yourself. I'm big into systemizing and putting systems into place to automate what you're doing. So that's also really important. But you can't have email sucking up all your time. It's absolutely critical that you do that.

And so the first one being focus, the second one being email, and the third one, I mean, you can kind of pick from a whole bunch of them. But the thing that I really like the most is this whole idea, and it goes along with focus but it's a little bit different, and it's the idea of doing time blocking. Which means that instead of saying I have 10 things to do today, I'm going to fit them in when I can, it's picking those top one, two or three items and actually blocking out your calendar where you focus on them and nothing else.

So take this call that you and I are doing right now. This is at 11 my time on a Tuesday, and it's obviously afternoon your time at 2. And so you and I both have this time blocked. And everybody who is listening to this call right now, either probably hearing it in their car or maybe they're hearing it at the gym, but they're actually listening to this in a block of time. And if you focus on something during that time block, you can get so much more done. And the key thing is to do it uninterrupted. I do it in at least 50-minute blocks, if not two- or four-hour blocks at a time. **And one of my good friends, who's a fighter pilot, says it's like a jet engine. Once you get spooled up working on a project, it's like a jet engine.** It goes faster and faster the more speed that you have. And it works better and more efficiently.

And if you get interrupted, so say that you're busy and you're working on a project, you're typing away, you're getting something done and it's productive and you're in the zone, and then somebody comes into your office, breaks your concentration and says, "I have an urgent thing. You've *got to look at this." You tell them to leave and now you've basically, and they've proven this, you just cost 20 minutes of productivity.*

So, you can't be interrupted during these time blocks, so one of my favorite exercises is the time-tracking worksheet. So take a worksheet out, take a blank piece of paper, put across the top Monday to Friday and put down the left side whatever time you start. So for Jim, it's going to be 4 a.m. For me it's going to be a little bit later, like 7 or 8. And you put until the end of the day, whatever that is for you, and you track your time in 15-minute blocks. And you'll find that the time you get the most done are when you block off time and nothing else gets in your way.

*And all the most successful people I've seen do this without exception. I haven't seen anybody that hasn't yet. And if somebody knows of somebody that doesn't, maybe Bill Gates doesn't do it. I don't know. But **everybody I've seen that is very successful has this concept of blocking time.***

Good scheduling is just a critical, critical piece. I mean, I always say that there's a lot of gold that comes out of smart people's mouths when they talk. But what you just said, there's a lot of gold in that. It's that you don't do your own schedule and that was something I started doing that recently, too. My assistant handles my schedule now and travel, admin, paperwork, booking flights. You have no idea how much time that stuff takes up. And so if you do that time-tracking and you see you've spent two hours trying to research the cheapest flight to go on a trip, you can pay somebody $10 or $20 a hour to do that and you can go focus on $1,000-an-hour work or whatever your income target is. It's so much better use of time.

JIM PALMER:

You talk a lot about learning in the book. I have an opinion on this, but do you ever come to a place where you say, OK, I've learned enough, and it's just time to do it, or what's your feeling on learning?

HENRY EVANS:

That is such a great question and I've actually asked the same question to people that are very, very successful. And so I've kind of adopted what they've said, and I'd be curious what your thoughts are too. My thought is that you have to take time to constantly sharpen your own saw. To kind of use the Stephen Covey analogy, it's like sharpening the saw. This means spending the time on the reading and the learning. **I find as I get more and more sophisticated as a marketer, I find it's OK, my marketing expertise is arguably from one of the best people in the world doing marketing now, because I've studied with Dan Kennedy and with Bill Glazer.** *I run their group out here in San Diego. And so I'm really very, very adept at doing marketing now, online, offline, whatever.*

So I find that I read more on mind-set and learning how to really harness the power of my mind and what I'm doing there, focusing on other skills that I want to add. So I definitely consider myself a very competent copywriter, but I'm constantly going through copywriting courses to learn more about that. I'm doing a lot of video marketing now. So I see the web TV show that you're doing and I'm strongly considering doing a web TV show.

So I think the answer is that you never stop. And anybody who is listening to this, who follows you, knows that that's how you are, too, because I've seen you. You're showing up to the conferences just like I am. We arguably don't have to go to those, but they're good to go to because **who knows what little gem of information you're going to get when you're always open to learning.**

So I think it's not an either/or. But at the same time, I usually reserve the evenings when I'm at home after the kids are in bed, that hour a day I used to spend working, I usually spend that now on educating myself. And then **I also will oftentimes spend the first hour of the day** *or the first half hour of the day, reading something really uplifting, or listening to something where I'm learning a new skill. So I'll do that either at the start or at the end of the day. But I usually do something every day and I've got four or five books I'm constantly reading.*

Or when I go to a seminar, I'm looking for the one good idea that I'm going to actually implement and do. And say that you went to that event and you did nothing else other than implement what you just said, that's going to help you get more customers, get more clients, make more and impact more people. So it can be one thing acted upon. I see people leave with 20 pages of notes when I do my monthly marketing summits here in San Diego. And they'll come to the meeting; I'll get great guest speakers. They'll walk out with a ton of stuff and I'll tell them, "Look, especially if you're new, you're going to be overwhelmed. That's OK. Pick one thing you're going to do."

And actually there's a guy in my group, he owns a store called Pair-A-Dice Games. He sells board games and role-playing games like Dungeons and Dragons and things like that. And his business was literally circling the drain, that is the terminology he uses. And he came to one of my meetings, started coming every month and decided that he was going to try to make this work.

*He'd already announced to his clients that he was closing the doors, he was shutting down. And so he started with one thing. **The very first thing he did was handwritten thank-you notes.** And he wrote a hand-written thank-you note to everybody that had ever bought anything from him, ever, who he had their physical address. That was the first thing he did. Then every month he just picked one thing to do and now he just, I think either doubled or tripled the size of his business. Super happy, saved three jobs, three families and everybody else who was impacted from that but it was just because he said, "I'm going to do one thing every month and do it to completion." And so, the same thing you just said. It's* *just critically important people constantly be learning and getting those new ideas because you never know which idea is going to be the million-dollar one for you.*

JIM PALMER:

I know you're a family guy. Does having two young kids impact you, and is there any reason they were part of writing the book? Is that part of your strategy?

HENRY EVANS:

*Oh, it's huge. It's a huge part and that was one of the biggest reasons why I left the corporate world is because I was capped on what I could make. I was in sales, I really wasn't capped, but there was a limit to what I could make just based on the number of hours I had in a day. I couldn't get much more leverage. I had a team of 12 people I was managing and I was there at the office every single day or I was on the road. And **I didn't want to be an absent chair at the dinner table. I really wanted to be able to spend time with my kids.** That was the major reason that pushed me to become so obsessed with time management and getting things done faster is because at the end of the day, I know that my two girls are going to be grown up like your kids are and out of the nest soon enough. And they're 7 and 8 right now, and it's going by fast.*

So I really want to make sure that I'm able to spend as much time with them as possible. I take them to school when I can in the morning. I pick them up when I can in the afternoon. We get together. We do the Indian Princesses, which is traveling with your kids and camping with them, which is just a phenomenal program through the YMCA if any dads or moms are listening to this. You can do that with your kids, it's fantastic. And so, yeah, that was actually one of the major reasons that I wrote the book, because at the end of the day I want to help other people live a better life so they can do what they want, when they want, with who they want. And for me, probably like you, I think it's one of the reasons that we get along is we're both really family guys at heart and that's where I wanted to spend more of my time and just everything I do just enables that to happen more often that's all.

JIM PALMER:

That's cool. You know what they say about asking a question you know the answer to. But I think it's a good question anyway. And I want to ask you about Mastermind groups. I know you talk a lot about Mastermind groups in your book. How important is it for entrepreneurs to be in Mastermind groups? I know you're running four different businesses. You're a very, very busy individual, but I know you're also in Mastermind groups. So talk about the power of Masterminding.

HENRY EVANS:

Single most important thing I've done to become successful without question is joining and being in Mastermind groups. *I think it was Jim Rohn, a very wise man, who had the saying that you're the sum total of the five people that you're associated with the most. And so, if all your friends are making $20,000 or $30,000 a year and playing video games every day after work, then that's what you're going to most likely end up at if you aren't already there. Likewise, if you hang out with people who are making a million dollars a year, you're going to gravitate toward them. And so when I learned that, it let me know that number one, I had to fire some friends and get some new ones, but also I wanted to be associated with people that were making things happen.*

And the first Mastermind group I joined was actually out in Tampa, Florida. And I joined this Mastermind group. It was I think around $15,000 and change, or $14,997 or something like that.

I joined it and I came home and told my wife that I was spending the equivalent of a new car with somebody I'd never met and I was going to be using up all of my vacation time to travel out to Tampa, Florida, to meet with this guy. So it went over like lead bricks to say the least. But I'll tell you what, doing that group, and I only did for a year mainly because of the travel. But it was a transformational experience and it exposed me to high-level people, making things happen, doing good things, while also making a great living at the same time.

And so it really opened the door for me. And since that time I'm actually personally involved in four Mastermind groups as a participant. Obviously, yours being one of those. I love your group. You've got phenomenal people that you surround yourself with. And so it's being around people that are making things happen and entrepreneurs who actually have a soul and a purpose. And those are the kind of people I like to hang out with.

And then I also run three groups myself here in San Diego. I have three full groups and a waiting list. And then I've had the good fortune of getting to know and become friends with Mike Koenigs and his partner, Rocket Helstrom, who run Traffic Geyser, which is a phenomenal company. And I've helped them with some launches, their affiliate programs in the past. And now I actually run two high-end Mastermind groups with them. So I'm partnered with them. The three of us run those two groups, which has been phenomenal because they attract very high caliber people. We actually had John Assaraf speak last week to our Mastermind group of less than 20 people, which is just amazing.

So I think the single most important thing anybody listening to this can do is get involved in a Mastermind group, ideally one that's run by somebody that knows what they're doing and has experience with it. And the first thing I ask anybody who is running the Mastermind group is, how many Mastermind groups are you in because what you don't want is the person that thinks they already know everything so they don't have to be in them anymore themselves. And you want smart people regardless of income, it's just a mind-set. They're in them because they know it's going to help them get to the next level regardless of where they are. So, single most important thing I've done and I always recommend it to people that I meet who are wondering how to get where they want to go on the success track. And being in a group like that, having a peer group that supports you, and cares about you, and wants you to succeed, and is pulling for you, and is going to give you shortcuts and ideas and techniques and strategies and contacts and resources to get there. I mean, it's just been incredible. So, I'd be curious how that's impacted you, too, because I know that you feel the same way on that too, Jim.

JIM PALMER:

Oh, my gosh, you know, when I got in my first Mastermind group, I forget what the investment was. I think it was like $350, $400 a month, something like that. It was six, seven years ago. And it was big dollars for me right then, and I can't even believe the impact immediately because I always have been an implementer, good work ethic. But the ideas and hanging around other people who are doing it and making it happen was motivating. And I think one of the biggest things I love about Mastermind, both being in a group and also leading a group, is the accountability factor because when you tell people in the group you're going to do something, and when people tell me they're going to do something, as you know, I typically say, "When are you going to have it done by. By the time we meet next month, will you be able to share the results?" They're like, ahhh.

So nobody wants to come back like the second month in a row not having done it. So go back to your analogy when we started the call about the Friday before vacation. I don't care if you're getting it done the night before the next Mastermind call, you're getting it done and you're moving forward. And that is a great thing.

HENRY EVANS:

Yes. I've had that happen too.

JIM PALMER:

Yeah, 60 days later I launched No Hassle Marketing, and it just wasn't the right thing at the right time. But I never would have had that idea had it not been for a Mastermind group, so very, very powerful. We have maybe five, six minutes left in the call. I always love giving people a chance to talk about their business, how people can learn more about you, certainly how they can find out more about your book. So the floor is yours, Henry. What can you tell everybody?

HENRY EVANS:

Sure. Well, if anybody happens to be in the San Diego area, they're welcomed to come to one of my local meetings. We have one of the biggest and best Glazer-Kennedy groups anywhere, and so you can find out more about that at www.timezonemarketing.com. You can get information on the local groups there.

And then my book website, which should be up by the time people are listening to this, is called www.houradaybook.com, so h-o-u-r-a-d-a-y-b-o-o-k.com, so houradaybook.com. And there'll be a ton of resources on there. You can obviously get a copy of the book. And so I'm really excited for that. And we'll have a bunch of freebies on there. Free videos, you can actually get a tour of my office and see some of the systems that I'm actually using. I'm real big on not hiding anything.

You see a lot of people who teach marketing and do coaching and stuff where you feel like they're always keeping the good stuff behind the curtain. I'm very transparent. So I'll actually show you how my office is set up and how my swipe files are set up and things like that. I actually have videos that walk you through that. So there's some real high-value content on there that you can actually take and use to make your own business more successful. So based on when people get this, that site should be up and they're more than welcomed to check that out, and let me know what they think about the book. I'd love to hear the feedback on it.

JIM PALMER:

That's awesome. And anybody listening to the call, Henry is high quality, very honest, ethical. He does what he says. I spoke at his chapter meeting out there. It's a really cool chapter. I know what California traffic can be like, but if you're within an hour of San Diego, you've got to go to the Glazer-Kennedy chapter meeting in San Diego. It's a very, very well-run meeting. I've spoken at more than 25 individual Glazer-Kennedy meetings, and I would put that certainly up at the top three, probably, as far as the number one, the quality of the meeting you run, Henry. But also the quality of the people in that chapter is so impressive. I mean, wow, it's really cool. I definitely want to encourage everybody to get a copy of the book. Henry, I'm like you. I also subscribe to the pull back the curtain, be open and transparent.

HENRY EVANS:

Well, thanks for having me on the call, Jim. I mean I really value my relationship with you. And I just think that you're just a phenomenal person, not even counting the fact that you're a great marketer and you have great tools and systems. I've been using your newsletter techniques and tactics, and I have all of your templates for the local IBA groups and I started that. And I've been doing it for it'll be two years this July and haven't missed a month, because I didn't want to be a newsletter pansy, *and that's a physical printed newsletter that's mailed to almost 1,000 people here in my local market. But I've learned a lot from you. I really value your friendship and I've really tried to give people some things they can take, walk away with. So I hope people got some good strategies and ideas on how to get more done and the whole concept of an hour a day. And I hope they check out the book because there's even more in there that we didn't even have a chance to cover. So thanks again for the opportunity.*

JIM PALMER:

My pleasure. And what a great way to end the call, talking about an hour a day. I think we just spent a good hour right there. So look what you can get done in an hour, folks!

Free bonuses with this book

Visit www.HourADayBook.com

As an owner of this book, you are entitled to a *free, three-part video training* and audio recording of this book worth $550. In these videos, I personally walk you through the best resources to use on your journey to business and entrepreneurial success.

This *free* video training includes short, powerful videos where I will share my secrets with you – no theory here, just hard-hitting and impactful strategies you can use immediately that cover:

- A walk through my personal Top 5 online resources for entrepreneurial success

  □ You will learn how to leverage your time
  □ Perform quick and thorough research
  □ Stay motivated even when life and business are bringing you down
  □ Systematize your team and operations
  □ Stay organized. How to keep your files up to date.

- A secret "best practices" technique that will help you easily maintain life balance and achieve true peace of mind

- Your own copy of the **daily checklist that I've designed and refined over nearly two decades living and winning in the trenches of the real world**

- Ever wonder exactly how to do what everyone says you should be doing regarding testing? I'll explain what you need to know without any fluff in this short video tutorial on testing.

And you'll get the "**Double Your Time Back**" secret I use nearly every day.

All of these resources are *free* and yours just for asking. Grab them now, because I don't know how long they will be available on the website below.

Visit www.HourADayBook.com to get your FREE gifts today.

Printed in the USA
CPSIA information can be obtained
at www.ICGtesting.com
JSHW012025140824
68134JS00033B/2885